LOCOMOTIVE

· PORTFOLIOS ·

GREAT WESTERN

STAR CLASS

LOCOMOTIVES

GREAT WESTERN
STAR CLASS
LOCOMOTIVES

LAURENCE WATERS

PEN & SWORD
TRANSPORT

First published in Great Britain in 2017 by
Pen & Sword Transport
An imprint of Pen & Sword Books Ltd
47 Church Street
Barnsley
South Yorkshire
S70 2AS

ISBN 978 1 47387 102 1

Design and typesetting by Juliet Arthur, www.stimula.co.uk

Printed and bound by Imago Publishing Limited

Pen & Sword Books Ltd incorporates the imprints of Pen & Sword
Archaeology, Atlas, Aviation, Battleground, Discovery, Family History,
History, Maritime, Military, Naval, Politics, Railways, Select, Social History,
Transport, True Crime, and Claymore Press, Frontline Books, Leo Cooper,
Praetorian Press, Remember When, Seaforth Publishing and Wharncliffe.

For a complete list of Pen & Sword titles please contact
Pen and Sword Books Limited
47 Church Street, Barnsley, South Yorkshire, S70 2AS, England
E-mail: enquiries@pen-and-sword.co.uk
Website: www.pen-and-sword.co.uk

ACKNOWLEDGEMENTS

The images used in the book are taken from a number of collections that have been left to the Great Western Trust, and are now kept in the new archive building at Didcot Railway Centre. The collections of the late P.J. Reed and C.G. Stuart provide a wonderful archive of early twentieth-century Great Western material. However, a number of the images used in the book are unfortunately devoid of any information other than the locomotive number. I have tried where possible to provide some additional information for these, including dates, locations, etc. But any errors are down to the author.

Individual locomotive details have been taken from the original Great Western locomotive records that were collated together by the late Bill Peto, and are now held by the Great Western Trust at Didcot Railway Centre. I have also consulted original internal Swindon Works documents relating to the both the testing and the naming of the Star Class.

The following publications have been very helpful: *Churchward Locomotives* by Brian Haresnape, *Great Western Saints and Sinners* by W.A. Tuplin, *An Outline of Great Western Locomotive Practice 1837–1947* by H. Holcroft, *The Great Western Stars, Castles and Kings* by O.S. Nock. Also the RCTS *Railway Observer* magazines 1932–1953, *Great Western and Western Region* Magazines 1903–1953, the *Locomotive, Railway, Carriage and Wagon Review*, and various Great Western operating timetables of the period.

I would like to thank L.A. Summers for his help with the manuscript, and Professor C. Tuplin for allowing me to use his late father's sectional Star drawing. The R.C. Riley image is courtesy of R. Lissenden.

Picture Credits: every effort has been made to identify and correctly attribute photographic credits. Should any error have occurred this is entirely unintentional.

Laurence Waters,
Oxford, 2016

THE GREAT WESTERN STAR CLASS 4-6-0S

Churchward's four cylinder Star Class 4-6-0s were, for many, years the crack performers on Great Western main line services. They were loved by footplate men and enthusiasts alike, and although these superb free-running locomotives were gradually superseded by Collett's more powerful Castle and King Class 4-6-0s, the Stars continued to give good service right up until the last working example, No. 4056 *Princess Margaret*, was withdrawn on 28 October 1957.

George Jackson Churchward was born in Stoke Gabriel, Devon, on 31 January 1857. After leaving school he began his lifelong career on the railway with an apprenticeship on the South Devon Railway at the Newton Abbot works. On 1 February 1876, the South Devon Railway amalgamated with the Great Western; and in 1877, aged 19, Churchward moved jobs to Swindon, where he was initially employed in the Materials department. He was well thought of at Swindon, and in 1897 after successive promotions he ended up as the Chief Assistant to the then Locomotive Carriage and Wagon Superintendent, William Dean. Dean was not in good health at this time, and by 1898 Churchward was essentially running the Locomotive Department, although technically still Dean's assistant. Dean officially retired through ill health on 31 May 1902, and on 1 June, Churchward took over as head of the department.

Much of his early experimental work was centred on devising improvements in the design of the boiler and smokebox as well as the cylinders and valve gear, and also in the individual balancing of all coupled wheels, together with the introduction of lightweight big ends with solid bushes.

In the year before he officially took over from Dean, Churchward had outlined the need for up to six new 'standard' locomotive types that would meet the needs of the traffic department at that time and also of the potential growth in future traffic. Up to this point, Great Western motive power comprised mainly double frame locomotives with the cylinders placed inside the frames. Churchward's concept was for a series of simple expansion engines with single frames, using Stephenson valve gear, and with the cylinders placed on the outside of the frames. These six new classes' new locomotives would have standardised cylinders measuring

George Jackson Churchward.
(Great Western Trust)

18 inches in diameter with a 30in stroke, plus 8½in piston valves together with a standardised valve motion, and just two main types of boiler.

The first on his list was a heavy main line express locomotive with 6ft 8½in driving wheels. It is well known that Churchward had been a great admirer of both American and European locomotive design. American locomotives tended to be simple and basic with high running frames, as opposed to the rather more sophisticated designs of the European locomotives, particularly those running in France. He particularly admired the French 4 cylinder De Glehn compound 4-4-2s, which at this time were considered to be some of the finest express passenger locomotives in Europe. Churchward was to eventually incorporate some of best features of these locomotives into his own designs, but not the compound system, which he had dismissed from an early date. In order to effect a comparison with his own Saint prototypes that were still very much in the development stage, he had persuaded the Great Western to purchase at a cost of about £4,000 a De Glehn Atlantic from the *Society Alsacienne de Constructions Mechanique* of Belfort. The locomotive was placed in Great Western stock in October 1903. Numbered 102 and named *La France*, it had 6ft 8½in coupled wheels and a boiler that was similar in size to the Swindon No. 1 boiler, but which operated at a slightly higher pressure of 227lb psi. In 1905 a

further two De Glehn Atlantics were purchased by the company, again for testing purposes, being numbered 102 and 103 and named *President* and *Alliance* respectively. Interestingly these three French locomotives, although altered over the years by the Great Western, ran on express services until their withdrawal in 1926, 1927 and 1928 respectively.

In 1902, No. 100, the first of three prototype 2 cylinder Saint class 4-6-0s, with 6ft 8½in coupled wheels, left the factory at Swindon. This unique locomotive was followed by Nos. 98 and 171 in March and December 1903. The importance of these 2 cylinder locomotives cannot be underestimated as they set the standard for express power on the GWR and elsewhere in both performance and design until the advent of the Stars. The history and development of these fine locomotives are described in detail in my book *The Great Western Saint Class 4-6-0s*.

With the success of the Saints, Churchward now turned his attention to producing an even more powerful 4-6-0 again with 6ft 8½in driving wheels, but this time with 4 cylinders. Construction of a 4 cylinder simple express passenger locomotive (No. 40) had been authorised by the Great Western Board on 19 July 1905, at an estimated cost of £3,600, but it was not until a year later that the prototype appeared. The engine record sheets show that its actual cost was £3,219 for the locomotive and an extra £1,036 for 3,500 gallon tender No. 1654. Churchward's

various reports to the Directors make interesting reading. He first mentioned the construction of his 4 cylinder prototype in a report to the Directors dated 5 December 1905 regarding the construction of the 2 cylinder Saint Class 4-6-0s. He states: 'The engine (No. 40) is not yet complete. It is designed with four small simple cylinders with a view to see if the same smoothness of running and economy can be obtained as with the De Glehn compounds without the same amount of complication and cost.' He goes on to say: 'I had hoped to postpone the construction of any more heavy express engines until No. 40 had been tested but it is now found that to provide a margin for working heavy services next summer, we should have another ten engines of maximum power. I am recommending a vote for ten of the 4-6-0 class for this purpose (the Saints).'

In April 1906, No. 40 finally emerged from the works as a 4-4-2, and after extensive testing was allocated to Old Oak Common on 20 June 1906. On 29 June 1906 in yet another report Churchward states, 'This engine has now been at work for a week or two and the result is very promising indeed.' This report is interesting as he also gives his reason for eventually abandoning the 4-4-2 wheel arrangement: 'It (No. 40) is reported to be more powerful than any of our other engines and to run with remarkable steadiness at high speeds. If we build more of them, I think it will be necessary on account of the great power, to couple six wheels, as the

A works shot of Star prototype No. 40, as built in April 1906 as a 4-4-2 Atlantic. It is pictured here with a long cone No. 1 boiler, which operated at 225lb psi pressure, a small diameter copper capped chimney and a swing link bogie. It has square drop ends and fluted coupling rods and the works plate mounted on the front splasher. Notice also the sand box mounted just ahead of the front splasher, and the circular hole in the front frame to give some access to the inside valve gear. It was named *North Star* in September 1906. Here it is coupled to Churchward 3,500 gallon tender No. 1654, which was built especially for No. 40.

amount of slipping with four wheels is more than it should be for good practice. From our experience now with engines of this power it is clear that we must couple six wheels and this limits the possible types to 4-6-0 or 4-6-2.'

In September 1906, No. 40 was named *North Star*. Although the 2 cylinder Saints were an important step in Great Western locomotive design, it could be argued that No. 40 was probably even more important as it set the standard for all Great Western 4 cylinder express passenger locomotives for years to come. In its initial configuration No. 40 was built as a 4-4-2 Atlantic, again for testing purposes. In this form it had 6ft 8½in coupled wheels,

four 14¼in diameter cylinders and a 26in stroke, and was fitted with a long cone example of the Swindon No. 1 boiler with a working pressure of 225lb psi. This boiler had a tube heating surface of 1,988.65sq ft and a firebox heating surface of 154.26sq ft, giving a total heating surface of 2,142.91sq ft, which gave a tractive effort at 85% of 25,090lbs. In operating condition the locomotive weighed in at 74 tons 12cwt, plus another 40 tons for a 3,500 gallon tender, making a total of 114 tons 10cwt. No. 40 differed from the later Stars in that it was fitted with a scissors type valve gear to operate the four cylinders. This gear, although simple in design, was apparently difficult and time

consuming to set up and mainly for this reason was abandoned in favour of a specially designed Walschaerts valve gear.

The problem of setting up the scissors gear was summed up many years ago in an article published in the *Great Western Echo* by J.C. Gibson who was a member of the valve setting team at Swindon A shop. He relates that: 'the job of setting the scissors gear was extremely difficult and protracted owing to the necessity of taking down the inaccessible scissor-blade arms and links for smithing something like three or four times during the operation, which often took ten days or more instead of a day and a half which was usual for other types of

An as yet un-named No. 40 is pictured here near Acton, probably in July 1906, with the down Cornish Riviera Express. This was a regular turn for No. 40 at this time. (Great Western Trust)

gear. This could be endured for one locomotive (No. 40), as it was for some twenty years, but was obviously an intolerable disadvantage for a large class, the first examples of which must have been on order almost as soon as No. 40 had finished its early trials, since they entered service only ten months later.'

In service, however, No. 40, with its scissors gear, proved to be a good and reliable performer putting in some exceptional runs. It soon became apparent that the fluted coupling rods fitted to No. 40 were not strong enough, being replaced by the much stronger standard rectangular pattern rods. No. 40 had apparently bent the fluted rods on at least one occasion whilst in a slip.

As mentioned previously, Churchward had already abandoned the 4-4-2 arrangement after deciding that the greater adhesive weight of the 4-6-0s meant that they were better suited to Great Western services, particularly over the undulating gradients in the south west. On 12 August 1909, No. 40 entered Swindon works where it was rebuilt as a 4-6-0, after travelling some 119,888 miles as a 4-4-2. Whilst in the works it was fitted with new frames and the wheelbase was shortened by about 6 inches to conform to later batch built locomotives. It was also given curved drops ahead of the cylinders and the cab side sheet was taken down with a similar curve replacing the previously sharply angular pattern. The rectangular box casing over the inside cylinders was replaced by the later curved pattern first fitted to No. 4021. Interestingly the footplate height, which was 2½in higher than the other Stars, remained the same. In December 1912 the locomotive was

A view of No. 40 at Plymouth shows it running with the later type standard full cone boiler and top feed. Its sand box has now been moved from the running plate to between the frames.
(Great Western Trust)

Another superb shot of 4-6-0 No. 40 *North Star*, pictured here near Twyford on the up Cornish Riviera.
(Great Western Trust)

renumbered No. 4000, and apart from a number of boiler changes it retained the scissors valve gear right up until its conversion to a Castle in November 1929, after which it was fitted with Walschaerts valve gear.

Its dimensions as built were:

Cylinders	4	
Diameter	14¼in	
Stroke	26in	
Boiler		
Barrel	14ft 10in	
Dia outside	4ft 10¾ in and 5ft 6in	
Pitch	8ft 6in	
Firebox length outside	9ft 0in	
Heating surface		
Tubes	1,988.65sq ft	
Firebox	154.26sq ft	
Total	2,142.91sq ft	
Grate area	27.07sq ft	
Boiler pressure	225lb	
Tractive effort (at 85%)	25,090lb	
Wheels	4-4-2	
Bogie	3ft 2in	
Coupled	6ft 8½in	
Trailing	4ft 1½in	
Wheelbase	7ft 0in+5ft 6in+7ft 0in+8ft 3in = total 27ft 9in	
Weights		
Bogie	17 ton 18cwt	
Leading coupled	19 ton 16cwt	
Trailing coupled	19 ton 16cwt	
Trailing	17 ton 0cwt	
Total	74 ton 10cwt	
Tender (capacity 3,500 gallons)	40 ton 0cwt	
Total	144 ton 14cwt	

After the success of No. 40 the Great Western built the first ten of its famous Star class locomotives in 1907, numbered 4001–4010. Unlike No. 40 they were built as 4-6-0s, and were named after some of the old broad gauge Star class 2-2-2s. Churchward referred to the construction of these in a report to the Directors dated 4 June 1907: 'We have now seven of the ten four-cylinder engines at work, and from the results up to the present, it appears that they will probably be very successful. Their hauling power on gradients is certainly greater than anything that we have yet employed, and, as far as can be judged, their coal consumption will not be more than the four cylinder compounds. The 10th engine of the lot will be fitted with a superheater, which I trust will further reduce the consumption of coal.'

This batch was slightly cheaper to construct than No. 40, being costed at £3,180 for the locomotive and boiler plus an extra £483 for the tenders, which were built in batches, unlike No. 1654 which was a one off. The scissors valve gear fitted to No. 40 had now been abandoned and all were fitted with Walschaerts valve gear from new (although they may have originally been ordered with the troublesome scissors gear). The long travel Walschaerts gear was set between the frames, with the two independent sets of gear being operated via two large eccentrics that were mounted on the leading coupled axle. The valves of the two outside cylinders were operated by two horizontal cranked levers.

Nos. 4001 and 4002 were built with long slots in the slidebars, and No. 4010 *Western Star* was built as an experiment with an American-designed Cole superheater. All were fitted with screw operated reverse and now had a square hole cut into the frame plate over the bogie to allow access to the piston rod, gland and cross head.

The new locomotives differed in appearance to No. 40 in that they had the framing curved at both drop ends. Curved drop ends had been first introduced on the Saint Class after widespread criticism of their angular look, notably by James Stirling of the Great Northern Railway. W.A. Tuplin relates in his book *Great Western Saints and Sinners* that this design change was apparently suggested by H. Holcroft, who was at the time a member of the technical staff at Swindon. The suggested change in design, Tuplin concluded, 'would be an attempt to soften the visual angularity of the early Saints', and that the subsequent result would, 'look as if somebody at Swindon had actually bothered about their appearance'. On the Stars the look was further enhanced by the uncluttered long cone boilers, tall safety valve bonnets and the tall narrow copper capped chimneys. All ten locomotives were fitted with the early type of swing link; this was essentially an American design with the loads being applied to the axlebox by equalising bars. To achieve this two springs were fitted parallel to the equalising bars, and which transmitted the load from the

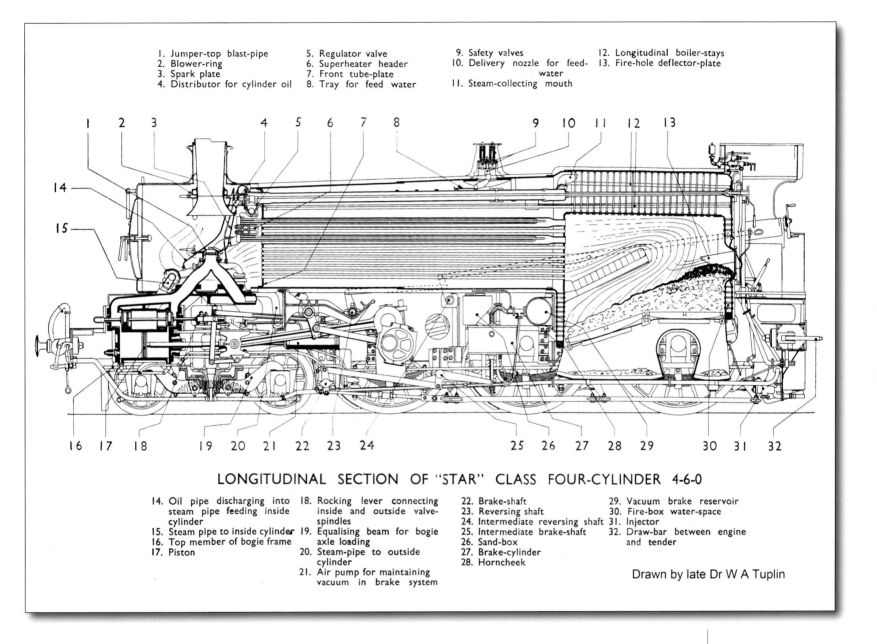

1. Jumper-top blast-pipe
2. Blower-ring
3. Spark plate
4. Distributor for cylinder oil

5. Regulator valve
6. Superheater header
7. Front tube-plate
8. Tray for feed water

9. Safety valves
10. Delivery nozzle for feed-water
11. Steam-collecting mouth

12. Longitudinal boiler-stays
13. Fire-hole deflector-plate

LONGITUDINAL SECTION OF "STAR" CLASS FOUR-CYLINDER 4-6-0

14. Oil pipe discharging into steam pipe feeding inside cylinder
15. Steam pipe to inside cylinder
16. Top member of bogie frame
17. Piston

18. Rocking lever connecting inside and outside valve-spindles
19. Equalising beam for bogie axle loading
20. Steam-pipe to outside cylinder
21. Air pump for maintaining vacuum in brake system

22. Brake-shaft
23. Reversing shaft
24. Intermediate reversing shaft
25. Intermediate brake-shaft
26. Sand-box
27. Brake-cylinder
28. Horncheek

29. Vacuum brake reservoir
30. Fire-box water-space
31. Injector
32. Draw-bar between engine and tender

Drawn by late Dr W A Tuplin

A superb sectional drawing by W.A. Tuplin showing the workings of a Star Class 4-6-0.
(Courtesy Professor C. Tuplin)

frame to the bars, the bogie being connected to the frame by swing links. Unfortunately this type of bogie proved to be unsatisfactory in service and the swing links were troublesome, causing excessive wear to both pivots and flanges.

The dimensions of the first ten were:

Cylinders		4
	Diameter	14½in
	Stroke	26in
Boiler		
	Barrel	14ft 10in
	Dia outside	4ft 10¾in and 5ft 6in
	Pitch	8ft 6in
Firebox length outside		9ft 0in
Tubes		250, diameter 2in
Heating surface		
	Tubes	1,988.65sq ft
	Firebox	154.26sq ft
	Total	2,142.91sq ft
Grate area		27.07sq ft
Boiler pressure		250lb
Tractive effort (at 85%)		25,090lb
Wheels		
	Bogie	3ft 2in
	Coupled	6ft 8½in
	Wheelbase	7ft +5ft 6in+7ft+7ft 9in = total 27ft 3in
Weights		
	Total locomotive	75 ton 12cwt
	Tender	40 ton
	Total	115 ton 12cwt

The second batch of Stars, the Knights, was completed in 1908 and again comprised ten locomotives. The first of these, No. 4011 *Knight of the Garter,* was the first to be fitted with a Swindon designed No. 1 field-tube type superheater, and although satisfactory in service this was replaced by what became the new Swindon standard No. 3 design in 1910. Another innovation introduced on the Knights was a new improved bogie comprising side control springs and side bearers in place of the old swing links. The new type of bogie fitted from No. 4011 onwards was a Churchward variation of the French De Glehn bogie. On this design the swing links were discarded and replaced by side control springs and side bearers, although the equalising bar was retained. This effectively reduced flange wear and lessened the tendency of lateral movement of the front end. The new bogies were eventually fitted to all of the earlier Stars. Nos. 4002/08/09/11–16 and 4018 were fitted with footsteps just ahead of the cylinders, but it was soon realised that these caused an access problem to the inside motion and were soon removed.

The third batch, Nos. 4021–4030, the 'Kings', was built in 1909. On these the square box casing over the inside cylinders was curved at the edges giving a more graceful front end appearance. No. 4021 became the first Star to be fitted from new with what became the standard Swindon No. 3 superheater. Interestingly, the other nine were all built with non-superheated saturated boilers of various dimensions. Between October 1910 and March 1911, a further ten

No. **4008** *Royal Star* (LA) pictured here, probably at Old Oak Common. It has the narrow copper capped chimney, tall safety valve bonnet, long cone boiler and curved drop ends to the frame. (Great Western Trust)

No. 4010 *Western Star* (PDN), pictured here, probably soon after construction at Old Oak Common. When built, No. 4010 was fitted with an experimental Cole superheater, but this was replaced by the standard Swindon version in 1909. (Great Western Trust)

Diagram of Star Class as fitted with No. 1 boiler and top feed. (Great Western Trust)

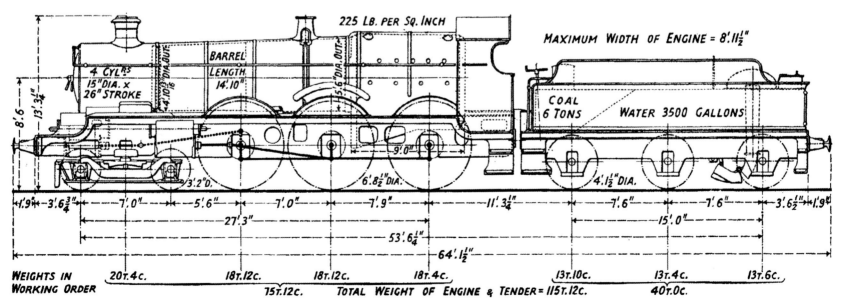

Stars, Nos. 4031–40, were constructed at Swindon and named after English queens. They were all fitted from new with the Swindon No. 3 standard superheater. For these ten locomotives the Great Western built brand new 3,500 gallon tenders with the longer side fenders.

Official view of cab of No. 4012 *Knight of the Thistle*. Notice the large and somewhat awkward positioned screw reverser on the right.
(Great Western Trust)

The next batch to be built was the five 'Princes', Nos. 4041–4045; these were completed in June 1913. All five were fitted with standard No. 1 boilers, complete with Swindon No. 3 superheaters and top feed. Top feed had been introduced by Churchward in 1911 and resulted in a considerable reduction in maintenance costs. With the superheaters the tube heating surface was raised to 1,599.4sq ft, the firebox to 155.0sq ft and the superheater to 260.0sq ft, making a total of 2,014.4sq ft. This, together with the new larger cylinders, had the effect of raising the tractive effort (at 85%) to 27,800lb.

In June 1913, initially as an experiment, No. 4041 was built with 15in diameter cylinders instead of the normal 14¼in diameter, the aim being to match the increased cylinder diameter with the higher output of the superheated boiler. The success of this experiment saw the 15in cylinders become standard for the whole class.

Nos. 4042 and 4044 were built with steel fireboxes. Some twenty-four members of the Star Class are known to have carried half cone boilers at various times from 1909 to 1921, although none was built with one. Records show that these boilers had originally been used on the Saint Class, but for use on the Stars they had been fitted with superheaters and top feed.

Between May and July 1914 another fifteen Stars were constructed at Swindon. These were the 'Princesses' and were numbered 4046–4060. By this date many of the earlier modifications had already been introduced, and all fifteen came out with 15in cylinders, superheaters and top feed. They were the first Stars to be fitted with the large external 4 cone ejectors, recently introduced by the Company as a standard fitment on all of its larger passenger locomotives.

The final batch of Stars comprised twelve locomotives, Nos. 4061–4072; all were built under Collett's regime in 1922/23 and were named after abbeys on the Great Western system. This batch had improved balanced crank axles, and Nos. 4061/62/67–72 were fitted with fluted coupling rods. Another change that was introduced from Star No. 4051 saw the screw reversing lever moved further forward in the cab from the previous awkward position. Moving it forward gave the driver a more comfortable

stance. All of the Abbeys were turned out in austerity livery comprising cast iron chimneys and plain green paint, with the brass beading removed from the splashers. Interestingly the cost of building a Star had gone up considerably from the £3,180 of No. 4001 in 1907 to £7,516 (including the boiler) of No. 4061 in 1923. The cost of tender construction had also risen from £483 to £1,276.

Over the years the seventy-three members of the class underwent many modifications, some taking place during construction but many others whilst the locomotives were in service. Between 1919 and 1924, as and when they went through the works, twenty of the early members of the class were also fitted with the austerity cast iron chimneys. However, between 1925 and 1927 and with an improving situation, the pre-war lining was once again restored and the cast iron chimneys were gradually replaced by the standard larger type with copper caps. From around 1927 the class were gradually fitted with shorter safety valve bonnets, and also, for the first time, whistle shields were fitted to prevent drifting steam obstructing the view from the round cab spectacle windows. One wonders just how effective these windows were as it seems that from around 1928 they were being gradually removed from the class.

All of the class had been fitted from new with bogie brakes but in everyday use these proved to be less than reliable and were maintenance heavy. Although they were considered to be ineffective, for whatever reason Churchward would not allow their removal, but as soon as Collett took over he ordered tests to ascertain their usefulness. Testing soon took place, both with and without the bogie brakes in operation, and it was soon found that they had little effect, and from November 1923 they were gradually removed. From around 1929/30 the front bogie was simplified ever further with the introduction of better and more flexible springs that allowed the removal of the spring equalising gear.

Also during this period the appearance of many members of the class was substantially altered with the fitting of outside steam pipes. Two types of pipes were fitted, the 'elbow' and the 'Castle' patterns. The elbow type was required when new inside cylinders or saddles were fitted in conjunction with the old type outside cylinders. The elbow pipe doubled back acutely between the frames, and No. 4002 was the first to be fitted with these, in December 1929. The second pattern was the Castle pipe; this had less of an angle and was fitted to members of the class that received the new Castle pattern outside cylinders. No. 4024 was the first to receive this type, in February 1929. Two Stars actually carried both patterns: No. 4048 had elbow in 1932 and Castle in 1938; and No. 4060 had elbow in 1930 and Castle in 1944.

From around 1932 the top lamp brackets were removed to a lower position on the smokebox, and although No. 4050 had been fitted with an early design speed recorder in 1914, speed recorders were not fitted to other members of the Star class until around 1937. It is interesting to compare the 4 cylinder Stars with the 2 cylinder Saints in terms of mileage run between general repairs. It seems that whereas the Saints could run on average for between 70,000 and 80,000 miles between repairs, the Stars could considerably increase this figure to an average of 120,000–150,000 miles, although as years went on and with improved maintenance and servicing, the gap between the two classes narrowed. W.A. Tuplin admirably summed up the outstanding capabilities of Churchward's 4-6-0s as 'an excellence in basic design matched by excellence in detail, workmanship, and maintenance, as well as driving and firing'.

In 1923 Collett introduced his Castle Class 4-6-0s, which were based on the Star Class and were essentially an enlarged Star. In service the Castles were proving cheaper to maintain than the Stars and to that end Collett decided to rebuild some of the Stars into Castles.

Between 1925 and 1929 five members of the class, Nos. 4000/09/16/32/37, were rebuilt as Castles as and when they visited the works for cylinder replacement. The work involved basically entailed not much more than fitting new Castle Class cylinders and cabs. Why only five? Probably by this date the number of new Kings and Castles in service were sufficient to handle the heaviest trains so further conversions were really not required. However, between 1937 and 1940 ten of the Abbeys, Nos. 4063 to 4072, were withdrawn from service, again as and when they required new cylinders. These ten locomotives were renewed under Lot No. 317 as members of the Castle Class, in the same order but renumbered 5083–5092. Although essentially rebuilds, they were considered by Swindon to be new engines, hence the new numbers. All retained their names after conversion but a small 'Castle Class' plate was mounted under the Abbey names.

Names

The Great Western naming policy in the early 1900s was strange to say the least, with the two new Churchward 4-6-0 classes, the 4 cylinder Stars and the 2 cylinder Saints, being given a variety of names. Of the Star class only eleven locomotives were named after stars, with the rest named after knights, kings, monarchs, queens, princes, princesses and abbeys. The 2 cylinder Saints were even more diverse, being named after saints, ladies, courts, Company Directors, books, characters from Walter Scott novels, and even a racehorse. It took Collett to introduce some sort of cohesion into the Great Western naming policy, with (Castles excepted) the King, Hall, Grange and Manor classes. Although it must be said that naming a class after Halls that eventually totalled some 330 locomotives was perhaps a bit monotonous.

The prototype Star No. 40 (later 4000) was given a favourite Great Western name, *North Star*. This name was carried by no fewer than four Great Western types between 1837 and 1957. The name was first carried by the broad gauge 2-2-2 built by Robert Stephenson & Co at Newcastle in 1837; it was the first

An early shot of No. 4003 *Lode Star* (PDN) at Old Oak Common. It is fitted with the Churchward version of the French De Glehn bogie. It has the early type square cover over the cylinders, T-section slide bars with a tie rod between them and an early type tender with short side fenders.
(Great Western Trust)

A close up showing nameplate and works plate of No. 4004 *Morning Star*. The works plate carries the following information: engine No. 4004 built February 1907, and Swindon works No. 2232.
(Great Western Trust)

locomotive on the Company's books, and was withdrawn in January 1871 after which it placed in store at Swindon. Surprisingly it was broken up under Churchward's orders in February 1906, just a few months before No. 40 was constructed.

As mentioned earlier the remaining Stars were constructed in seven batches. The first batch was Nos. 4001–4010 in 1907 which were named after stars and planets. All of the star names were first used on the broad gauge Star class 2-2-2s, with the exception of *Bright Star*. The name *Load Star* was chosen for No. 4003 but was altered to the later spelling *Lode Star*. Interestingly, three of the names all relate to the same heavenly body (the North Star). No. 4003 *Lode Star* is an alternate name for Polaris (the North Star) and No. 4005 *Polar Star* is also an alternate name for the North Star (Alpha Polaris). Two of the other names are related to planets: No. 4005 *Morning Star* relates to the planet Venus, and No. 4006 *Red Star* is another name for the planet Mars.

The next batch built in 1908, Nos. 4011–4020, were named after knights. On this batch the nameplates were considerably larger than those of the rest of the class and differed from others in that they had concave ends to the lower backplates. Some idea of the size of these plates can gleaned from the fact that two of the names, *Knight of the Black Eagle* and *Knight of the Grand Cross,* each comprised twenty-one letters, while the longest of the Knight names, No. 4016 *Knight of the Golden Fleece* comprised twenty-three letters, and is, I believe, the largest single line name ever carried

by a Great Western locomotive. (The nameplate fitted to Castle No. 5017 *The Gloucestershire Regiment 28th,* 61st in April 1954, was similar in style to the Knight plates, but the thirty-four letters and numbers were actually spread over three levels).

No. 4014 *Knight of the Bath* became the source of some humour as it was known for many years by railwaymen and enthusiasts alike as 'Friday night'. For those readers too young to remember, for many in this country Friday night was bath night.

The Knights were followed in 1909 by Nos. 4021–4030 named after kings of England, and these were in descending order starting with the reigning monarch, *King Edward.* Unfortunately, it then went slightly wrong as *King Henry* and *King Richard* were reversed.

Nos. 4031–4040 were constructed in 1910/11 and were named after

English queens, starting with *Queen Mary* and once again in descending order back to *Queen Boadicea*, but in the process missing out quite a number of queens. These were followed two years later in 1914 by Nos. 4041–4045, the Princes, named after the five sons of King George V. The largest batch to be built, also in 1914, were the fifteen Princesses, Nos. 4046–4060. The late Bill Peto concluded that the names were 'picked from a general roundup of English Princesses that were still extant in 1914'.

The final batch of twelve was constructed under Collett's regime, being turned out during 1922/23. Nos. 4061–4072 were named after abbeys on the Great Western system. In regards to naming the Great Western often got things wrong, as Nos. 4066 *Malvern Abbey* and 4068 *Llanthony Abbey,* of which ruins still

An official shot of No. 4016 *Knight of the Golden Fleece* at Swindon in April 1908, as built with non-superheated boiler. This batch was constructed with improved bogies with side control springs and side bearers in place of swing links.

(Great Western Trust)

Great Western internal memorandum concerning the accent on the nameplate of No. 4017 *Knight of Liége*.
(Great Western Trust)

exist, are technically not abbeys but priories as they were under the control of a prior not an abbot. No. 4066 *Malvern Abbey* retained its name until May 1935 when it was renamed *Sir Robert Horne*. This was later changed to *Viscount Horne*, then it was withdrawn from service in December 1937 for conversion to a Castle. Rather surprisingly, probably the best-known abbey, Westminster, was omitted from the list, but after some correspondence between the public and Swindon regarding this omission,

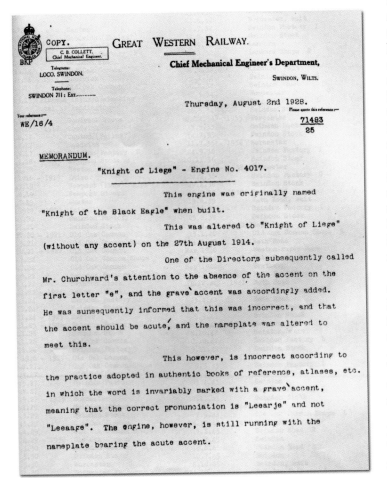

No. 4069 *Margam Abbey* (which actually was an abbey) was renamed *Westminster Abbey* in May 1923.

From quite early on a certain amount of re-naming and other alterations took place. In August 1914, and because of its German connotations, the name of No. 4017 *Knight of the Black Eagle* was removed and replaced by *Knight of Liege*. It was soon pointed out that Liege should have a grave accent over the 'e'. This was duly done, but the addition of the grave accent generated a good deal of correspondence on the subject, which resulted in the grave accent being removed and replaced by an acute accent. After further correspondence this was also deemed to be wrong, but I would imagine that by this time Swindon were fed up with the subject and No. 4017 retained the acute accent above the 'e' as *Knight of Liége* until its withdrawal. The problem, it seems, is that the grave accent is correct in French, but the acute accent is correct in Flemish (Belgian Dutch). I have included out of interest a Swindon internal memorandum on the subject.

During the First World War, and as an austerity measure, the brass beading was removed from around the splashers on all of the Stars built up to that date (Nos. 4000–4060). After hostilities ceased the Great Western went through a period of austerity and sadly the beading was never replaced.

On 28 February 1922 Princess Mary married the Earl of Harewood. The obvious locomotive to haul the royal wedding train, No. 4046

Princess Mary, was in the middle of a Heavy repair at Swindon, so the GWR did one of its famous swaps, putting the nameplates from No. 4046 onto fellow class member No. 4048 *Princess Victoria*, which ran on the day as *Princess Mary*. I would imagine that the Great Western ensured that the royal couple knew nothing of the ruse.

The construction of the thirty Collett King class 4-6-0s between June and August 1927 saw the King nameplates removed from the Stars. A Swindon memorandum dated 10 May 1927 states, 'that the King names be removed and replaced by Monarchs'. No. 4021 was named *The British Monarch* in June 1927, and another nine foreign monarchs followed. The name *The Egyptian Monarch* was apparently chosen for No. 4024 but this was dropped prior to naming and replaced by *The Dutch Monarch*. Within just a few months '*The*' was removed from all (except No. 4025, which had been named just *Italian Monarch*). The reason is for the removal of '*The*' is explained in another internal memo dated Monday, 10 October 1927 from R.G. Harrington which states, 'that there has been much criticism of the length of names in this series and it can be considered that the plates would be much better if the word "*The*" were omitted and the spacing rearranged.'

In May 1937 No. 4007 *Rising Star* was re-named *Swallowfield Park*, the one-time home of Charles Russell, third Chairman of the GWR from 1839–1855. His descendants still reside there today. After the outbreak of war and during 1940/1 the nameplates carried by Nos. 4022 *Belgian Monarch*, 4023 *Danish Monarch*, 4025 I*talian Monarch*, 4026 *Japanese Monarch*, 4028 *Roumanian Monarch* and 4029 *Spanish Monarch* were all removed and replaced by the words 'Star Class' painted on the centre wheel splasher. After the war these six locomotives were never re-named and ran like this right up until their withdrawal in the early 1950s. Of the others, Nos. 4024, 4027 and 4029 were all withdrawn in 1934/35, but No. 4021 *British Monarch* for obvious reasons retained its name until its withdrawal on 10 October 1952.

Livery

Prior to the First World War, Stars were turned out from new in Great Western fully lined green livery, with copper-capped chimneys and brass beading around the splashers. But during and after the First World War the lining was omitted and the brass beading removed. On many locomotives the copper caps were painted over and the safety valve bonnets were painted green. During this period Swindon started to use snap head rivets in place of countersunk rivets on the smokeboxes, cabs and tenders of its locomotives. The round head was apparently both stronger and cheaper and, more importantly, easier to remove. From 1919 some twenty Stars were fitted with tapered cast iron chimneys, but from around 1923 they were replaced by the larger copper-capped Castle design. During the interwar period

Nameplate of No. 4018. These large 'Knight' plates had concave ends to the lower backplates.

Nameplate of No. 4049.

Nameplate of No. 4007. Originally named *Rising Star*, it was renamed *Swallowfield Park* in May 1937.

'Star Class' as painted on the middle splasher of Nos. 4022/23/25/26/28/30 after they had their nameplates removed during 1940/1.

the Stars reclaimed much of their former glory, being fully lined out once again; unfortunately the pre-war look was not fully achieved as the brass beading around the splashers was never replaced. During the Second World War a number of Stars were painted in unlined black, although quite a number apparently went through the hostilities without any sort of repaint. After national-isation in 1948, as they went through the works the Stars were turned out in fully lined BR express passenger livery. Some forty-seven members of the class passed into Western Region ownership, but just one member of the class, No. 4062, received the short lived 'W' suffix under the cab number plate, used to denote a Western Region locomotive. A number had 'BRITISH RAILWAYS' painted on the tender, but this again was short lived when the new BR Lion and Wheel Emblem was adopted.

Their appearance was altered again with the removal of the large painted locomotive number from the front buffer beam, the introduction of cast iron smokebox number plates, and later on shed code plates. Seven members of the class, Nos. 4004/12/17/19/26/30 and 4045 were withdrawn from service without receiving either. These oval shed identification plates were fitted to the lower smokebox door from February 1950 with the exercise being completed by 1951. On 15 November 1950 whilst on an official visit to Swindon, HRH Princess Elizabeth 'drove' Star No. 4057 *Princess Elizabeth* from the works to the station. In November 1951 in commemoration of

the event, a small rectangular brass plate was fitted above the left-hand number plate. I wonder if she was aware that No. 4057 *Princess Elizabeth* was actually named after Queen Victoria's grand-daughter who was murdered by the Bolsheviks after the Russian revolution in 1918.

Tenders

The prototype No. 40 *North Star* first ran with tender No. 1654, which was constructed at Swindon in May 1906 especially for No. 40 and cost £1,036. In their early days the remaining Stars ran with the standard Churchward 3,500 gallon tenders, all of which were fitted with the shorter side fenders. From around 1910 as they went through the works these tenders were fitted with extended fenders. The batch of ten Stars that were completed in 1910/1 were coupled from new with 3,500 gallon tenders Nos. 1786–1795; all had the extended fenders. Many of the class ran with these 3,500 gallon tenders until their withdrawal, and records show that the average cost of these tenders was around £500. Several members of the class also ran with Churchward 4,000 gallon tenders that had been built between 1900 and 1904. However, starting from 1932 a number of Stars were being coupled to the standard Collett pattern 4,000 gallon tenders, No. 4060 *Princess Eugenie* being the first to receive one when it was attached to tender No. 2590 on 11 March 1932. After the Second World War these tenders became a standard fitment on the Stars. An interesting entry on the engine record sheet shows that on 29 August 1936, Star No. 4045 was coupled to Churchward's *Great*

Bear double bogie tender No. 1755, but that this was replaced on the same day with Churchward 4,000 gallon tender No. 1518. What is interesting is that tender No. 1755 had been officially withdrawn nine days earlier on 20 July 1936. One can only conclude that as Star No. 4045 had just left the works after an Intermediate repair the tender was probably being used as a temporary 'works' tender in order to move locomotives out of the works. It was cut up at Swindon on 17 October 1936.

The unique Collett 8 wheeled 4,000 gallon tender No. 2586, which was constructed at Swindon in August 1931, was coupled to Star No. 4043 *Prince Henry* between 6 February 1950 and 22 June 1950. Interestingly, this tender ended up coupled to Hall No. 5904 *Kelham Hall,* being withdrawn together with the Hall in November 1963. All of the Stars that survived into British Railways days finished up running with Collett 4,000 gallon tenders. Four members of the class ran at various times coupled to the Hawksworth design 4,000 gallon straight sided tenders. No. 4036 *Princess Elizabeth* was coupled to No. 4013 in 1948, and again with tender No. 4016 in 1950, No. 4053 *Princess Alexandra* with No. 4015 in 1950, and No. 4058 *Princess Augusta* with tender No. 4049 in June 1949 until its withdrawal in April 1951. Lastly, No. 4062 *Malmesbury Abbey* was coupled to no less than three of these Hawksworth tenders during its final years in service: tender No. 4056 from April to May 1950; No. 4014 from April 1952 until January 1953; and finally No. 4046 from July 1955 until the withdrawal of the locomotive in November 1956.

Star Workings

The Class were always known by the footplate staff as 'free running' locomotives and were used on many of the Great Western's fast services, being the ideal locomotive for long fast runs. For quite a number of years a large number were allocated at Old Oak Common and Plymouth. The engine record sheets show that in June 1913, out of the forty-six Stars in traffic, some twenty-four were at Old Oak and a further fourteen at Plymouth Laira, three were at Wolverhampton Stafford Road, three at Cardiff Canton and interestingly two at Goodwick. For many years the Stars were associated with working the Great Western's flagship service, the 'Cornish Riviera Express', which was at the time the world's longest non-stop run. Mr D.J. Warren, the Locomotive Department Foreman at Plymouth Laira, kept detailed records of locomotives that worked this service during 1912. These show that nineteen individual members of the Star class were used over this period on a total of 256 occasions.

In August 1910 No. 4005 *Polar Star* undertook exchange trials on the LNWR. In return the LNWR supplied a Whale Experiment Class 4-6-0, No. 1471 *Worcestershire*, to work services on the Great Western. Both locomotives were unsuperheated, and the subsequent results showed that No. 4005 was superior to No. 1471 in almost every way. It is said

that the superiority shown by the Star resulted in the LNWR commissioning the construction of the Bowen-Cooke designed Claughton Class 4 cylinder 4-6-0s. These were fitted with Belpaire fireboxes and Walschaerts valve gear but looked nothing like their Great Western counterparts.

The Stars had proved that they were quite capable of handling heavy loads at speed, as demonstrated by Old Oak Common allocated No. 4013 *Knight of St Patrick,* with Driver Morgans on the footplate. On 8 April 1914, the Wednesday before Easter, it hauled the midnight Paddington to Penzance service, comprising nineteen bogie coaches, from Bristol to Exeter in even time. On the following Bank Holiday, Monday, 13 April, the same locomotive, again with Driver Morgans in control, hauled the 6.27pm service, comprising seventeen bogie coaches, from Weston-super-Mare to Paddington, again in even time.

No. 4005 *Polar Star* (PDN) departs from Euston on the 10.00 am service to Carlisle on 28 August 1910. It was taking part in exchange trials with LNWR Experiment class 4-6-0 No. 1471 *Worcestershire.* No. 4005 is seen here with the larger diameter chimney and the French type bogie. Notice also that the slide bars have a tie rod between them, and that the Churchward tender is fitted with full length side fender.
(Great Western Trust)

No. 4000 *North Star* (PAD)	5 single journeys
No. 4003 *Lode Star* (PAD)	19 single journeys
No. 4005 *Polar Star* (PAD)	12 single journeys
No. 4006 *Red Star* (PAD)	10 single journeys
No. 4007 *Rising Star* (PAD)	18 single journeys
No. 4010 *Western Star* (LA)	15 single journeys
No. 4012 *Knight of the Thistle* (LA)	24 single journeys
No. 4015 *Knight of St John* (LA)	12 single journeys
No. 4016 *Knight of the Golden Fleece* (LA)	5 single journeys
No. 4018 *Knight of the Grand Cross* (PDN)	1 single journey
No. 4020 *Knight Commander* (LA)	25 single journeys
No. 4030 *King Harold* (PDN)	3 single journeys
No. 4031 *Queen Mary* (PDN)	12 single journeys
No. 4032 *Queen Alexandra* (LA)	12 single journeys
No. 4033 *Queen Victoria* (LA)	7 single journeys
No. 4036 *Queen Elizabeth* (LA)	25 single journeys
No. 4037 *Queen Philippa* (LA)	22 single journeys
No. 4039 *Queen Matilda* (PDN)	16 single journeys
No. 4040 *Queen Boadicea* (PDN)	12 single journeys

During the early 1920s the bulk of the seventy-three Stars in service at this time still saw extensive use on the west of England services, and were distributed thus: thirty-seven at Old Oak Common, fifteen at Laira, nine at Newton Abbot and one at Exeter. The remaining eleven were all at Stafford Road for use on the west Midland services.

Collet took over from Churchward in January 1922, and in August 1923 the first of his more powerful Castle Class 4-6-0s left the works at Swindon. The Castles can well be described as an enlarged Star, and by 1927 some forty-five were in traffic. Included in this number were four of the Star Class, Nos. 4009/4016/4026 and 4032, which were rebuilt by Collet as Castles during 1925 and 1926. (No. 4000 was not converted to a Castle until August 1929.) The Castles were soon put to use on the west of England services and by the early 1930s had almost completely displaced the Stars on these services. The allocation records for June 1930 show there were just twelve Stars at Old Oak Common, six at Exeter, and one at Laira. Of the remainder there were seventeen at Bristol Bath Road, nine at Wolverhampton Stafford Road, seven at Shrewsbury, and eight at Worcester. In South Wales another three were at Cardiff, two at Carmarthen and one at Landore. It was during this period that the Stars started to take over many of the Saint turns on services to South Wales, Worcester, Bristol and Shrewsbury. From about 1935 they also were reported as operating many of the secondary services emanating from Bristol, Weymouth, Oxford, Swindon, Birmingham and Wolverhampton.

Apart from the five members of the Class that were withdrawn during the 1920s for conversions to Castles, the first withdrawals proper came with Nos. 4006 and 4011 in November 1932; this was followed by eight more, Nos. 4001/02/05/08/10/24/27/29, between 1933 and 1935, all apparently being withdrawn due to being 'surplus to requirements by the Traffic department'. All ten were replaced by newly built Castle Class locomotives. Between February 1937 and October 1940, ten of the Abbeys, Nos. 4063–4072, were withdrawn for conversion to Castles. Probably because of wartime locomotive shortages no Stars were withdrawn during the Second World War, and only one, No. 4014 in June 1946, was withdrawn prior to nationalisation in 1948. The Stars that remained were still capable of good performances and continued to form a major part of the Great Western's locomotive fleet. They saw extensive use on the heavily loaded fast services on the north west route between Shrewsbury and the south west, but apart from the occasional fill in, they had essentially been displaced on an ever-increasing number of services by the Castles and Modified Halls.

In June 1950 the remaining forty-three members of the class were distributed thus: two at Old Oak Common, six at Swindon, ten at Bath Road, three at Westbury, one at Taunton, one at Oxford, seven at Stafford Road, five at Shrewsbury, one at Worcester, one at Gloucester, one at Chester, and five at Landore. By now they were operating mainly secondary parcels and freight services, and by this date the surviving members of the class had all completed in excess of 1½ million miles in service; many were essentially worn out. Swindon records show that at this time locomotives were withdrawn for a number of reasons, ranging from cracked frames and cylinders, cylinders bored out to their limit, boiler problems, even badly worn tyres, or just being surplus to requirements.

1951 was a bad year for the class with fifteen examples being withdrawn, including No. 4003 *Lode Star,* which luckily was set aside for preservation; another casualty was No. 4007 *Rising Star,* one of the first batch to be constructed. Eleven more were withdrawn in 1952 and four in 1953, which meant that in 1954 there were only four members of the Class still running, 4053/4056/4061 and 4062. This number was quickly reduced to just three with the withdrawal of No. 4053 *Princess Alexandra* on 12 July 1954. What is interesting is that the remaining three all had Heavy Classified repairs at Swindon during 1954–1955. No. 4056 *Princess Margaret* received a Heavy Intermediate repair in September 1955, No. 4061 *Glastonbury Abbey* underwent Heavy General repair in April 1955, and No. 4062 Malmesbury Abbey received a Heavy General repair in April 1954. No. 4062 was withdrawn on 5 November 1956, No. 4061 on

11 March 1957, and last of all No. 4056 on 28 October 1957. Towards the end of their working life two of the surviving Stars had been in demand for specials. On 11 September 1955 the Stephenson Locomotive Society used No. 4061 on its 'Star Special' Birmingham to Birmingham circular tour to Swindon Works via Stratford-upon-Avon and Cheltenham, returning via Didcot and Oxford. A year later on 9 September 1956 the Society again ran a 'Star Special' from Birmingham back to Birmingham via Hereford, Severn Tunnel Junction, Swindon and Stratford-upon-Avon, this time hauled by Bristol Bath Road based No. 4056. The same locomotive was used once again on 22 September 1956 on the Paddington to Shrewsbury leg of the Talyllyn Railway Preservation Society AGM special from Paddington to Towyn. Interestingly, for these tours both 4056 and 4061 had their numbers painted on the front buffer beams once again, in true Great Western style, although for a while both locomotives continued to run with their BR smokebox number plates and shed plates still intact.

As already mentioned the last Star to be withdrawn was Bristol Bath Road based No. 4056 *Princess Margaret*. Its last month or so in service makes rather sad reading. On Saturday, 7 September 1957 it worked the 12.30 pm service from Newquay to Paddington, and on arrival was reported to be in a deplorable state with the driver's repair card full of items for attention. On the following Monday, 9

September, it was booked to haul the 8.05 am Paddington to Bristol freight, but the failure of a Castle that was booked to haul the 7.15 am fast service to Bristol saw No. 4056 used instead. It could not have been steaming well as it was reported as stopping for a blow up at Ealing and then failing completely at Southall where it was taken off. On 16 September 1957 it apparently failed again, this time in Wales, as it is shown on the record sheet as being stopped at Landore. Here it stayed until it arrived at Swindon on 27 September. It was not repaired and was withdrawn on 28 October 1957, after running a total of 2,074,338 miles in service.

Luckily a very early example of the Star class, No. 4003 *Lode Star*, built at Swindon in February 1907 has been preserved. It was withdrawn from service on 18 July 1951 after running 2,005,898 miles in

service. The decision to preserve *Lode Star* had actually been taken by the Western Region some months earlier on 13 February 1951. For many years it could be seen in store in the stock shed at Swindon. It was always a static exhibit as it had its elbow steam pipes removed at Swindon some years earlier. In June 1962 it was placed on show in the newly opened GWR Museum at Swindon, and in March 1992 it was transferred to the National Railway Museum at York where it can be seen today.

I saw all of the remaining three Stars working, and can well remember seeing Wolverhampton Stafford Road-based No. 4061 *Glastonbury Abbey* on numerous occasions at Oxford, on Paddington to Birmingham services via Oxford, and also on the through cross-country service from Hastings to Wolverhampton.

No. 4003 *Lode Star* Stands in the yard at Swindon on 22 July 1951. It was withdrawn just a few days earlier on 18 July and is still coupled to Collett 4,000 gallon tender No. 2410. The tender was subsequently removed and the locomotive was placed in store, together with Collet 3,500 gallon tender No. 1726. (E. Mountford/Great Western Trust)

Preserved Star No. 4003 *Lode Star* is seen here on a low loader outside the Great Western Railway Museum at Swindon on Sunday, 29 April 1962. Because of the length of the load it proved to be a tricky manoeuvre to place it into the museum building, a converted chapel.
(E. Mountford/Great Western Trust)

I can find no reference to any of the Stars being involved in any fatal accidents during their lifetime and apart from the usual, mainly trivial, accidents involving loco crews, and the odd shed derailment, the following are worth mentioning.

An unusual occurrence took place on 6 April 1908 when it was reported that the driver of No. 4011 *Knight of the Garter* accidently reversed under steam whilst running between Goring and Didcot, with the result that one of the driving wheels shifted on the axle. The same locomotive was once again 'in the wars' when on 15 October 1908 it apparently fell into the turntable pit at Bath Road shed.

However, a more serious accident took place on 8 November 1924 when the driver of No. 4033 *Queen Victoria*, in foggy conditions, ran past signals at danger at Harwell Street sidings, just north of Plymouth Millbay. The locomotive subsequently derailed, falling down an adjacent bank. No one was seriously injured, and after retrieval the locomotive was towed back to Swindon for repair.

The most serious accident that I can find involving a Star took place on 8 January 1930 when No. 4063 *Bath Abbey*, hauling the 2.40 am service from Shrewsbury to Penzance, comprising nine eight-wheeled bogie coaches, was involved in a serious collision with the rear of the 3.55 am Stoke Gifford to Bristol East depot goods service, hauled by 0-6-0PT No. 2786, the collision taking place between

Stapleton Road and Lawrence Hill Bristol. Mr J.H.F. Burrough, the driver of the express, which at the time was travelling at approximately 45mph through Stapleton Road, luckily saw the tail lamps of the goods service and was able to slow the express down to about 20 miles per hour prior to the collision. Although a number of goods wagons and the brake van were destroyed, the guard jumped clear, and there were no major casualties. No. 4063 suffered front end damage and was taken to Swindon for repair.

On 1 April 1941 the driver of No. 4042 *Prince Albert* passed a red signal at Ladbrooke Grove near Paddington, derailing the locomotive, tender and first coach and demolishing the stop block and an adjacent high pressure gas reservoir.

During the Second World War No. 4047 *Princess Louise* suffered minor air raid damage at Weymouth on 17 January 1941, and on 16 April 1942 No. 4034 *Queen Adelaide* was machine gunned by an enemy aircraft at Dawlish. The damage sustained by No. 4034 was minimal and was repaired over a two day period at Exeter.

There is no doubt that the good safety record of the Stars can be put down to the introduction of the Great Western Automatic Train Control (ATC) together with the good working practices of the staff.

Shed Allocations
I have mentioned repair dates and other details such as tender numbers on a number of the photo legends. These have been obtained from the

official Great Western Star Class engine register sheets held at The National Archive at Kew. The classification of repairs are shown as follows:

Pre 1948: G = General, H = Heavy, I = Intermediate, L = Light, and R = Running repair.

Post 1948 the Western Region used the following descriptions: HC = Heavy Classified, HG = Heavy General, HI = Heavy Intermediate, LC = Light Casual, LI = Light Intermediate and U = Unclassified.

Locomotive allocations as used in the photo legends

Prior to nationalisation Great Western shed allocation codes were stencilled in the cab and later on

the locomotive side frame in front of the cylinders. Although some forty-seven members of the Star class passed into BR stock in 1948, probably only around forty were fitted with smokebox number plates and probably even fewer received the BR shed plates that were fitted to the lower smokebox door. In February 1950 the Western Region started to use these new shed codes, so for images taken after this date I have used the BR codes.

Stars were allocated at various times to the following locomotive depots:

PDN pre 1906	Westbourne Park
PDN post 1906	Old Oak Common (81A)
OXF	Oxford (81F)
BL	Bristol Bath Road (82A)
SWN	Swindon (82C)
WES	Westbury (82D)
WEY	Weymouth (82F)
NA	Newton Abbot (83A)
TN	Taunton (83B)
EXE	Exeter (83C)
PLY	Plymouth Laira (83D)/ Millbay
WSR	Wolverhampton Stafford Road (84A)
BAN	Banbury (84C)
TYS	Tyseley (84E)
SALOP	Shrewsbury (84G)
WOS	Worcester (85A)
GLO	Gloucester (85B)
HFD	Hereford (85C)
CDF	Cardiff Canton (86C)
LDR	Landore (87E)
CAR	Carmarthen (87G)
FDG	Goodwick (87J)

No. 40 was named *North Star* in September 1906 and converted to a 4-6-0 in November 1909, and is pictured here at Old Oak Common, probably soon after conversion. It has been fitted with new frames that have curved drops front and rear, and the circular access hole above the front bogie has now been enlarged to a rectangle. Note its Swindon works plate (No. 2168) is now mounted under the nameplate on the centre splasher, which also has the addition of brass beading.
(Great Western Trust)

No. 4001 *Dog Star* was the first of the production Stars. Built in February 1907, it is pictured here under test, and probably soon after its completion. Notice the test pipe running from the outside cylinder into the wooden indicator shelter. On this batch, and all subsequent members of the class, a large square hole was cut into the front frame plate over the bogie, to allow better access to the adjacent piston-rod, gland and crosshead.
(Great Western Trust)

No. 4008 *Royal Star* (LA), pictured here at Teignmouth, probably soon after construction in 1908, with an up mixed service comprising mainly of Dean stock.
(Great Western Trust)

An almost new No. 4024 *King James* (PDN), together with Bulldog 4-4-0 No. 3362 *Newlyn,* passes Dawlish with a down fast service in August 1909. The fact that the Star is at the front of the train may indicate that it is returning to its home depot instead of running light.
(Great Western Trust)

An early shot of No. 4028 *King John* (PDN) standing at Bristol Temple Meads, probably soon after construction in 1909. Notice that the tender has the short side fenders.

(Great Western Trust)

No. 4021 *King Edward* (PDN) is seen here at Old Oak Common, decorated for hauling the funeral train of King Edward VII from Paddington to Windsor on 20 May 1910. The side shields were draped in purple and it has the GWR royal train headlamps. Interestingly, the funeral was attended by no fewer than nine reigning European monarchs.

(Great Western Trust)

The funeral train itself, seen here passing Ealing on 20 May. Notice the fourth vehicle of the eleven-coach train is the rebuilt Queen Victoria's royal saloon.
(Great Western Trust)

Another shot of No. 4005 *Polar Star* as it speeds through
Kilburn and Maida Vale, with a Carlisle service during the
August 1910 exchange trials.

(Great Western Trust)

No. 4009 *Shooting Star* (LA) stands in the yard at Old Oak Common. Built in May 1907, it has been fitted with top feed and also has the wide pattern chimney. It was withdrawn from service in November 1924 and rebuilt as a Castle Class, re-entering traffic as a Castle in April 1925.
(Great Western Trust)

No. 4036 *Queen Elizabeth* was constructed at Swindon in December 1910 and is seen here in 1911 in pristine condition at its home depot in Plymouth.
(Great Western Trust)

An up fast service hauled by No. 4011 *Knight of the Garter* (LA), is pictured here entering Brent station in March 1912. The Knights were fitted from new with improved bogies with side control springs and side bearers in place of swing links.
(Great Western Trust)

The elegant lines of No. 4006 *Red Star* (PDN) can be seen to good effect as it receives attention at Plymouth North Road. The Churchward 3,500 gallon tender also has the short side fenders. (Great Western Trust)

No. 4017 *Knight of the Black Eagle* (PDN) passes through St Anne's Park on a Bristol to Paddington service, comprising, amongst others, some early Dean stock. The nameplates were removed in August 1914 and replaced by *Knight of Liége*. (Great Western Trust)

No. 4023 *King George* (PDN) is pictured here at Reading. It has the curved housing for the inside valve gear that was first introduced on this batch of Stars.
(Great Western Trust)

No. 4042 *Prince Albert* (LA) was built at Swindon in May 1913 and is pictured here at Plymouth Laira, probably soon after completion. The Princes were fitted with superheaters and top feed from new.
(P. J. Reed/Great Western Trust)

An undated official view of No. 4041 *Prince of Wales* on the turntable at Ranelagh Bridge. This rather cramped depot was opened as a servicing point in 1907; it provided watering and turning, but not coaling facilities. It remained open as a diesel stabling point until 1980. (Great Western Trust)

No. 4015 *Knight of St John* (BRD) is pictured here at Paddington, probably soon after its completion in March 1908.
(Great Western Trust)

No. 4036 *Queen Elizabeth* (WSR) is seen here after arrival at Birmingham Snow Hill. It is fitted with top feed and at this time carried a superheater damper cylinder on the side of the smokebox.
(Great Western Trust)

Pictured here at Plymouth is No. 4016 *Knight of the Golden Fleece* (PDN). For many years with its twenty-three letters this was the longest single line nameplate on the Great Western. It seems that this locomotive carried on a tradition for long names; it was rebuilt as a Castle in October 1925 and in January 1938 renamed *The Somerset Light Infantry (Prince Albert's)*.

(P. J. Reed/Great Western Trust)

The crew of No. 4013 *Knight of St Patrick* (PDN) pose for the photographer as it stands alongside the small loco shed at Henley on Thames, on 2 July 1914. It had worked in on a service from Paddington.

(P. J. Reed/Great Western Trust)

The 4.45 pm service to Worcester, hauled by No. 4017 *Knight of Liége* (PDN), is pictured here at Paddington on 5 July 1921. The nameplate on this Star was the subject of much correspondence (see main text).

(P. J. Reed/Great Western Trust)

A nice broadside shot of No. 4039 *Queen Matilda* (EX) at Plymouth Laira in the 1920s. It is fitted with the narrow type chimney and top feed. It still retains its bogie brakes; these were gradually removed from the Stars from November 1923. Notice also the three lamps stored on the front running plate.

(P. J. Reed/Great Western Trust)

A great shot of No. 4045 *Prince John* (WSR) with quite a mixture of stock, pictured here near Harbury with a Birmingham service, 1922.
(Great Western Trust)

No. 4037 *Queen Phillipa* (LA), pictured here at Plymouth. The Queens were fitted with standard Swindon superheaters, while the 3,500 gallon tenders had the extended side fenders.
(Great Western Trust)

No. 4053 *Princess Alexandra* (LA) is seen here at Plymouth North Road on 3 September 1921. It is in austerity livery with its safety valve bonnet painted over and the brass beading removed from the splashers.
(P. J. Reed/Great Western Trust)

A nice shot of No. 4065 *Evesham Abbey* on a west of England service. The Abbeys were the last batch of Stars to be built and incorporated all of the earlier modifications. No. 4065 was withdrawn in March 1939 and renewed as Castle Class No. 5085.

(Great Western Trust)

No. 4030 *King Harold* (WSR) is seen here near Kings Sutton with an up service to Wolverhampton. It was renamed *The Swedish Monarch* in July 1927, then *Swedish Monarch* in October 1927. (Great Western Trust)

In 1925 No. 4043 *Prince Henry* (WSR) was fitted with an experimental smoke box with the chimney moved to a forward position, and is pictured here at Old Oak Common on 29 August 1925. The arrangement was originally carried by No. 4060 between 1920–1923, then transferred to No. 4043, and in 1927 to No. 4004 *Morning Star,* after which the experiment was discontinued. (P. J. Reed/Great Western Trust)

A down fast service to Plymouth and beyond is seen here arriving at Exeter St Davids, hauled by No. 4049 *Princess Maud* (PDN).
(Great Western Trust)

No. 4000 *North Star* (WSR) is pictured here at Wolverhampton Low Level in around 1926. Notice that it has been fitted with the later type curved inside valve cover. In July 1929 it entered Swindon for a Heavy General repair, and whilst in the works it was fitted with Castle Class cylinders and a Castle Class cab, emerging on 27 November 1929 as a member of the Castle Class.

(Great Western Trust)

Looking spruced up with polished buffers is No. 4046 *Princess Mary* (NA) as it stands at Exeter St Davids with an up fast to London. This was the first of the 1914 batch of Stars, comprising fifteen locomotives. They were fitted from new with 15in. cylinders and large external 4 cone ejectors.

(Great Western Trust)

No. 4001 *Dog Star* (EXE) passes Newbury Racecourse in the late 1920s with a seven-coach down fast service. Notice that No. 4001 has been fitted with a whistle shield, a modification that was eventually applied to all of the Class. (Great Western Trust)

No. 4022 *King William* (LA) stands in the winter sunshine at Plymouth North Road on 12 November 1921. It is in austerity unlined green livery with the safety valve casing painted black and its brass beading removed. It was re-named *The Belgian Monarch* in June 1927.

(P. J. Reed/Great Western Trust)

No. 4014 *Knight of the Bath* (LA) is seen here at Exeter in around 1927. It has had its bogie brakes removed and is fitted with top feed. It had elbow steam pipes fitted in September 1935; notice the angular inside cylinder casing.

(Great Western Trust)

No. 4018 *Knight of the Grand Cross* (LA) makes a fine sight as it passes Twyford East Box with a down fast. The locomotive is in plain green livery and many of the coaches are in chocolate and cream. Twyford East Box was closed on 23 October 1961.
(Great Western Trust)

No. 4051 *Princess Helena* (PDN) stands inside the roundhouse at Old Oak Common. It has the tall type cast iron chimney and is fitted with top feed. This batch was fitted with 15in cylinders, and the more graceful curved housing for the inside cylinders can be seen to good effect. (Great Western Trust)

No. 4050 *Princess Alice* (PDN) is pictured here after arrival at Birmingham Snow Hill on 24 March 1922. (P. J. Reed/Great Western Trust)

No. 4001 *Dog Star* (PDN) is pictured here near Twyford on the second portion of the down Torbay Express. The locomotive has a cast iron chimney and has the box type casing over the inside cylinders.
(H. Gordon Tidey/Great Western Trust)

The down Riviera service is pictured here near Twyford, hauled by an immaculate
No. 4038 *Queen Berengaria* (LA).
(Great Western Trust)

An up fast service from Wolverhampton is seen here at Leamington in the summer of 1923, hauled by No. 4032 *Queen Alexandra* (PDN). No. 4032 was withdrawn on 7 December 1925 for conversion to a Castle.
(Great Western Trust)

No. 4029 *King Stephen* is pictured here in around 1926 at its home shed, Old Oak Common. It was re-named *The Spanish Monarch* in May 1927 and *Spanish Monarch* in October 1927. It was one of the five Stars that were withdrawn surplus to operating requirements during 1934.
(P. J. Reed/Great Western Trust)

No. 4048 posing as *Princess Mary* is seen here at Old Oak Common in February 1922. HRH Princess Mary married the Earl of Harewood on 28 February 1922 and the GWR Royal Train was required. No. 4046, the real *Princess Mary*, was in Swindon having a Heavy repair at the time so the Great Western temporarily placed its nameplates on No. 4048 for the occasion of the wedding.
(Great Western Trust)

The 11.15 am fast service to Bristol waits to depart from Paddington on 7 November 1924, hauled by No. 4033 *Queen Victoria* (PDN).
(P. J. Reed/Great Western Trust)

No. 4048 *Princess Victoria* (WSR) is pictured here on a Birmingham service taking water at Rowington Water Troughs. It has been fitted with a whistle shield and has had its bogie brakes removed. No. 4048 was fitted with new inside cylinders and elbow steam pipes in August 1932.
(H. Gordon Tidey/Great Western Trust)

An official picture of No. 4008 *Royal Star* (EXE), probably taken after a Heavy General repair at Swindon in August 1925. It is fitted with top feed and the bogie brakes have been removed. It was fitted with new inside cylinders and elbow steam pipes in July 1933, but was withdrawn from service on 1 June 1935.
(Great Western Trust)

A great shot of No. 4034 *Queen Adelaide* (LA) on the 4.30 pm
Plymouth service pictured, here at Tilehurst in May 1925.

(M. Earley/Great Western Trust)

No. 4016 *Knight of the Golden Fleece* (PDN) waits to leave Platform 1 at Paddington on 31 January 1925 with a fast service to Plymouth. It has been fitted with a whistle shield but still retains its bogie brakes.
(P. J. Reed/Great Western Trust)

No. 4022 *King William* (PDN) waits to depart from Paddington on 27 September 1925 with a service to Worcester. No. 4022 was renamed *The Belgian Monarch* in June 1927 and just *Belgian Monarch* in October 1927.
(P. J. Reed/Great Western Trust)

An undated view of No. 4034 *Queen Adelaide* (WSR) as it departs
from Paddington with a service to Wolverhampton.
(Great Western Trust)

No. 4017 *Knight of Liége* (WOS) awaits its next turn of duty at Old Oak Common in around 1927. Build as *Knight of the Black Eagle* it was re-named *Knight of Liége* on 27 August 1914.
(P. J. Reed/Great Western Trust)

Possibly the local inspector is seen here having a quiet chat with the driver of No. 4060 *Princess Eugenie* (NA) as it takes over the down Cornish Riviera Express at Plymouth in August 1926.
(Great Western Trust)

No. 4024 *The Dutch Monarch* (previously King James) receives attention as it stands outside Paddington in September 1927. Its name was altered to *Dutch Monarch* in October 1927.

(P. J. Reed/Great Western Trust)

No. 4028 *The Roumanian Monarch* (CDF) pictured here at Paddington on 10 July 1927. Originally named King John, it was renamed *The Roumanian Monarch* in early July 1927 and just *Roumanian Monarch* in November of the same year. The nameplates were removed in November 1940 and not replaced.

(P. J. Reed/Great Western Trust)

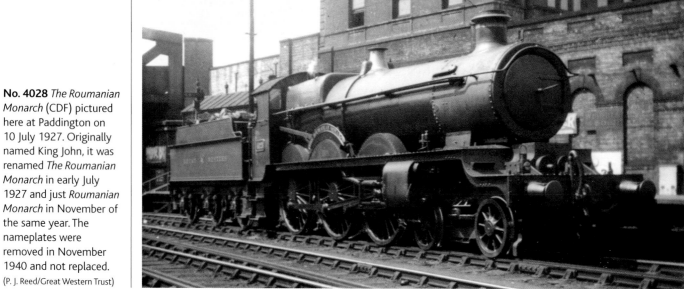

A permanent way gang stand and admire No. 4035 *Queen Charlotte* (LA) as it passes Twyford with a down service to the west of England. It was fitted with Castle pattern steam pipes in January 1931.
(Great Western Trust)

A down west of England service is pictured here near White Waltham, hauled by No. 4070 *Neath Abbey* (EX). It was fitted with elbow steam pipes in March 1937 and withdrawn and renewed as Castle No. 5090 in January 1939.

(Great Western Trust)

A shot of No. 4068 *Llanthony Abbey* (EXE), seen here at Swindon. It has the tall safety valve bonnet and cast iron chimney. It was withdrawn in November 1938 for conversion to Castle Class No. 5088.

(Great Western Trust)

A fast service from Paddington to Bristol and Weston-super-Mare is seen here passing Twyford East Box, hauled by No. 4064 *Reading Abbey* (PDN). It was withdrawn from service in February 1937 and rebuilt as Castle No. 5084.

(Great Western Trust)

A view of No. 4033 *Queen Victoria* (PDN), seen here with the Royal Train on the Shrewsbury to Hereford Joint line on 28 February 1923.
(Great Western Trust)

The crew of No. 4026 *The Japanese Monarch* (PDN) pose for the photographer in August 1927. Built as 4026 *King Richard*, it was renamed *The Japanese Monarch* in July 1927 and *Japanese Monarch* in October 1927. In this view it is coupled to Churchward 'Intermediate' pattern tender No. 2383.
(Great Western Trust)

The crew of No. 4034 *Queen Adelaide* (WSR) pose for the photographer at Tyseley. No. 4034 was fitted with elbow steam pipes in June 1932.
(Great Western Trust)

An up service from Weston-super-Mare and Bristol is pictured here near Iver (Bucks), hauled by No. 4013 *Knight of St Patrick* (PDN). The locomotive is fitted with top feed, and the spectacle plates have been removed from the cab.
(Great Western Trust)

No. 4069 *Westminster Abbey* (EXE) looks resplendent as it stands in Swindon A shop in August 1928 at the end of a Heavy General repair. It has the tall pattern chimney and safety valve cover and the bogie brakes have been removed.

(Great Western Trust)

No. 4008 *Royal Star* (EX) waits to depart from Paddington on 20 November 1928 with the 2.10 pm service to the south west. The awkward forward position of the screw reverser can be seen to good effect.

(P. J. Reed/Great Western Trust)

An undated view of No. 4067 *Tintern Abbey* is pictured here, probably on a Birmingham service. It has the tall cast iron chimney that was fitted to this batch from new. It was withdrawn from service on 14 September 1940 for conversion into a Castle, being re-numbered 5087. (Great Western Trust)

No. 4023 *Danish Monarch* (BRD) is pictured here approaching Bath with a down local service on 29 April 1930. It is coupled to Churchward 3,500 gallon tender No. 1741. Originally named *King George*, the locomotive was altered to *The Danish Monarch* in the summer of 1927, then to *Danish Monarch* in October of that year.
(Great Western Trust)

No. 4041 *Prince of Wales* (PDN) stands at Bristol Temple Meads on 26 April 1930. Notice in the background the Great Western luggage van with the inscription 'To work between Yeovil and Newcastle.'
(Great Western Trust)

The fireman of No. 4001 *Dog Star* (WSR) waits for the right of way with a down service to Wolverhampton on 14 June 1930.
(P. J. Reed/Great Western Trust)

The first of the five Princes that were built during May and June 1913 was No. 4041 *Prince of Wales* (BRD), pictured here at Weston-super-Mare in the early 1930s. This was the first Star to be fitted with 15in cylinders. (Great Western Trust)

A broadside view of No. 4063 *Bath Abbey* at its home shed in Exeter in July 1931. It had recently left Swindon after a General repair, where it was coupled to Collett 4,000 gallon tender No. 2531.
(Great Western Trust)

Over the years, Great Western always ran lots of interesting excursions and although not the sharpest of pictures, this shows No. 4002 *Evening Star* (PDN) at Paddington on 25 March 1932 with the 10.45 am Hikers Mystery Express No. 1.
(P. J. Reed/Great Western Trust)

No. 4019 *Knight Templar* (PDN) is seen here approaching Highbridge in September 1932 with a three-coach up stopping service from Taunton to Bristol. Withdrawn in October 1949, it was never fitted with outside steam pipes.

(Great Western Trust)

A side view of No. 4026 *Japanese Monarch* (PDN) is pictured here at Swindon, probably soon after being fitted with elbow steam pipes in October 1932.
(Great Western Trust)

No. 4027 *Norwegian Monarch* (Salop) stands in the sunshine at Plymouth Laira. Originally named *King Henry*, it was withdrawn from Swansea Landore in October 1934 having completed 1,121,371 miles in service.
(P. J. Reed/Great Western Trust)

A nice 1930's shot of No. 4033 *Queen Victoria* (BRD), seen here taking water at Goring Troughs on what is probably an up service from Bristol. No. 4033 was fitted with elbow steam pipes in April 1940.

(Great Western Trust)

No. 4005 *Polar Star* (PDN) poses for the photographer at Old Oak Common in the 1930s. Notice it has had its spectacle cab windows removed; these were gradually removed from the class from around 1925. No. 4005 was withdrawn from service 'surplus to requirements by the traffic department' on 17 November 1934.
(Great Western Trust)

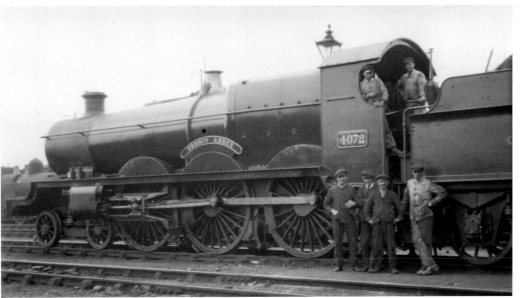

The last Star to be built was No. 4072 *Tresco Abbey* in February 1923. It is seen here in plain green livery, probably at Bristol Bath Road in the early 1930s. The Abbeys were turned out from new with improved balanced crank axles. No. 4072 was withdrawn for conversion to a Castle in December 1937.
(Great Western Trust)

No. 4048 *Princess Victoria* (EXE) is pictured here at Torquay as it waits to depart with an up stopping service.
(Great Western Trust)

Pictured here at Swindon in October 1933 is No. 4031 *Queen Mary* (Salop). It had just left the works after a Heavy Intermediate repair. It is painted in fully lined green livery and the snap head rivets which replaced the countersunk type can be seen to good effect. No. 4031 was fitted with elbow steam pipes in August 1948.
(Great Western Trust)

No. 4002 *Evening Star* (WSR) stands alongside the coaling plant at Old Oak Common in around 1932. It was fitted with elbow steam pipes in December 1929 and was withdrawn 'surplus to requirements' in June 1933.

(P. J. Reed/Great Western Trust)

Looking resplendent in fully lined green livery No. 4026 *Japanese Monarch* (EX) stands at Bristol Bath Road in November 1932. It had recently left Swindon where it had new inside cylinders and elbow type steam pipes fitted.

(Great Western Trust)

No. 4024 *Dutch Monarch* (EXE) stands at Newton Abbot in the summer of 1933 with a through service from Liverpool to Plymouth. In February 1929, it became the first Star to be fitted with Castle pattern outside cylinders and steam pipes. It was withdrawn from service in February 1935.

(Great Western Trust)

No. 4001 *Dog Star* (BRD) is pictured here at Old Oak Common on 17 June 1933. It was the only one of the first batch of Stars to be fitted with Castle pattern outside steam pipes. It was withdrawn from service on 1 January 1934.
(P. J. Reed/Great Western Trust)

A north to west service is seen here passing Craven Arms in March 1933, hauled by No. 4046 *Princess Mary* (Salop).
(Great Western Trust)

A down fast service speeds past the River Exe estuary at Powderham in August 1933, hauled by Exeter allocated No. 4045 *Prince John*. Notice the top lamp bracket has been moved to its lower position on the smokebox door.
(Great Western Trust)

No. 4008 *Royal Star* (PDN) awaits its next turn of duty at Swindon MPD on 10 September 1933. It had recently left the works where it was fitted with new inside cylinders and elbow steam pipes. Interestingly, it still retains the lamp bracket on the top of the smokebox. It was withdrawn 'surplus to requirements of the traffic department' on 1 June 1935.

(P. J. Reed/Great Western Trust)

No. 4015 *Knight of St John* (BRD) stands alongside the coaling plant at Old Oak Common in around 1934 when it was running attached to Collett 4,000 gallon tender No. 2359. The pipe on the side of the boiler is thought to be part of an experimental lubrication system.

(Great Western Trust)

No. 4033 *Queen Victoria* (WOS) awaits its next turn of duty at Oxford MPD on 21 April 1934. It has the tall chimney and safety valve bonnet and the top lamp bracket has been moved into its lower position. In the background is the ex-LNWR loco shed at Oxford Rewley Road.

(F. M. Gates/Great Western Trust)

An up fast service from Cardiff to Paddington is seen here at Patchway in around 1934, hauled by No. 4071 *Cleeve Abbey* (PDN).

(Great Western Trust)

Under dramatic skies, No. 4072 *Tresco Abbey* (BRD) is seen here at Wootton Bassett in April 1934 with a thirteen-coach up fast service from Bristol.
(Great Western Trust)

A broadside view of
No. 4051 *Princess Helena*
(Salop) as it stands at
Chester on 14 July 1934.
It was fitted with Castle
pattern outside steam
pipes in December 1944.
(R. Thomas/Great Western Trust)

A nice high level view of
No. 4004 *Morning Star*
(LDR), probably at
Cardiff Canton. It has the
tall chimney and safety
valve bonnet. Morning
Star is actually another
name for Venus, the
brightest Planet.
(Great Western Trust)

No. 4047 *Princess Louise* (LDR) receives attention at Swindon whilst in the works for a repair in June 1934, comprising amongst other things a change of driving wheels. (Great Western Trust)

A long parcels service from Shrewsbury is seen here arriving at Birmingham Snow Hill, hauled by No. 4058 *Princess Augusta* (Salop) on 4 September 1934. In the formation is a Great Western Royal Mail sorting coach.
(Great Western Trust)

No. 4057 *Princess Elizabeth* (PDN) is pictured here in the yard at Wolverhampton Stafford Road on 26 May 1935. It was fitted with Castle pattern outside cylinders and steam pipes in April 1930.
(M. Yarwood/Great Western Trust)

An interesting shot of No. 4025 *Italian Monarch* (Salop) on the turntable at Wolverhampton Stafford Road on 13 June 1935. It is coupled to Collett 4,000 gallon tender No. 2649. The nameplate was removed from this locomotive in June 1940.
(M. Yarwood/Great Western Trust)

A down semi-fast service, hauled by No. 4054 *Princess Charlotte* (EXE), rounds the curve at Dawlish in August 1935. It is running with Collett 4,000 gallon tender No. 2388.
(Great Western Trust)

No. 4018 *Knight of the Grand Cross* is pictured here, probably at Swindon. It was fitted with elbow steam pipes in May 1931 but still retains the upper lamp bracket.
(Great Western Trust)

A down Bristol local parcels service, hauled by No. 4045 *Prince John* (BRD), is pictured here at Hullavington in August 1935. It is coupled to Collett 4,000 gallon tender No. 2661.

(Great Western Trust)

No. 4014 *Knight of the Bath* (Salop) stands in the yard at Swindon on 10 September 1935. It had just left the works after a Heavy General repair where it was fitted with elbow type outside steam pipes. It has the lower safety valve bonnet and is coupled to Collett 3,500 gallon tender No. 2805, which has the full width fender and the newly introduced GWR roundel. This locomotive was, for many years, affectionately known as 'Friday night'.

(P. J. Reed/Great Western Trust)

No. 4071 *Cleeve Abbey* (SWN) is seen here at Swindon in around 1936. It is coupled to Collett 4,000 gallon tender No. 2265. It was withdrawn in September 1938 and renewed as Castle No. 5091.

(F. M. Gates/Great Western Trust)

A great shot of No. 4049 *Princess Maude* (WOS) is pictured here, fresh from a heavy general repair and in fully lined green livery at Swindon in June 1936. It was fitted with Castle pattern outside steam pipes in February 1935 and is coupled here to Collett 4,000 gallon tender No. 2621, which has the post 1934 GWR roundel.

(Great Western Trust)

A great shot of No. 4042 *Prince Albert* (BRD) on a down fast service to Bristol, picking up water at Goring Troughs in 1936. It is coupled to Churchward 3,500 gallon tender No. 1874.

(Great Western Trust)

Waiting to depart from Exeter St Davids on 4 May 1936, with a through service from Plymouth to Liverpool, is No. 4064 *Reading Abbey* (BRD). It is running here with Collett 4,000 gallon tender No. 2384. No. 4064 was rebuilt as a Castle Class in May 1937.

(P. J. Reed/Great Western Trust)

No. 4058 *Princess Augusta* (WSR) is seen here at Shrewsbury in the 1930s. It was fitted with elbow steam pipes in October 1944. The overall roof at Shrewsbury was removed in the 1950s. (Great Western Trust)

No. 4067 *Tintern Abbey* is seen here at Shrewsbury in around 1936. It was renewed as a Castle Class in September 1940 and numbered 5087. (Great Western Trust)

A nice portrait of No. 4023 *Danish Monarch* (LDR) as it stands in the yard at Cardiff on 19 May 1936. It has the short safety valve bonnet.
(F. M. Gates/Great Western Trust)

A nice portrait of No. 4054 *Princess Charlotte* (TN) as it stands at Plymouth North Road on 27 September 1936.
(Great Western Trust)

Another shot of No. 4014 *Knight of the Bath* (Salop) as it passes Patchway on a South Wales service in 1936.
(Great Western Trust)

No. 4022 *Belgian Monarch* (BRD) makes a fine sight as is passes Tram Inn on 2 June 1937 with a down North to West express service. The name *Belgium Monarch* was removed in May 1940.

(M. Yarwood/Great Western Trust)

A service to the South West is pictured here, probably at Dainton in the summer of 1937, double headed by No. 4055 *Princess Sophia* (BRD) and Castle Class No. 5031 *Totnes Castle* (WSR). (Great Western Trust)

No. 4014 *Knight of the Bath* (Salop) stands in the yard at Eastleigh in the late 1930s. It was fitted with elbow steam pipes in September 1935 and it is seen here with a short safety valve bonnet. It was withdrawn from service in June 1946. (Great Western Trust)

A nice view of No. 4004 *Morning Star* taking water alongside the old coaling plant at Oxford, its home shed, on 19 September 1937. It is coupled to Churchward 3,500 gallon tender No. 1834. Until a new coaling plant was built during the Second World War, all Oxford based tender locomotives ran with 3,500 gallon tenders.
(F. M. Gates/Great Western Trust)

Another Star on Southern territory. No. 4014 *Knight of the Bath* (SALOP) stands at Bournemouth shed in March 1938 after arriving with a through service from the West Midlands.
(Great Western Trust)

A great evening shot of No. 4038 *Queen Berengaria* (BRD) as it waits to depart from Paddington on 19 April 1938. It is pictured here coupled to Collett pattern 3,500 gallon tender No. 2258.
(L. Hanson/Great Western Trust)

No. 4030 *Swedish Monarch* (Salop) stands in the yard at Chester in May 1938. It is seen here coupled to Collett 4,000 gallon tender No. 2668. It was named *King Harold* until May 1937, then *The Swedish Monarch* for just a few months. Its nameplates were removed in November 1940 and not replaced.
(W. Potter/Great Western Trust)

No. 4018 *Knight of the Grand Cross* (WSR) stands under the overall roof at Shrewsbury with a Paddington service.
(Great Western Trust)

No. 4026 *Japanese Monarch* (TN) waits for its next turn of duty at Taunton in August 1938. It will take over an up fast service to London together with the single Siphon G van. Notice that it still has the high level lamp bracket.
(J Alves/Great Western Trust)

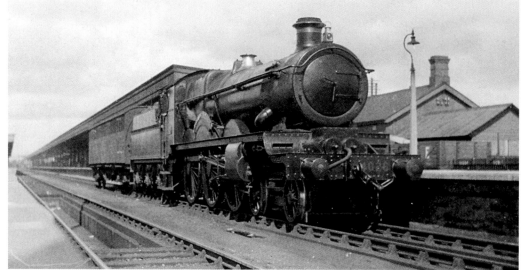

No. 4035 *Queen Charlotte* (BRD) is pictured here passing Thornford Bridge Halt on the Yeovil to Weymouth line with a down Weymouth service on 4 June 1939.

(M. Yarwood/Great Western Trust)

An up fast service from Bristol to Paddington is seen here at Wantage Road on 17 June 1939, hauled by Swindon based No. 4030 *Swedish Monarch*. The first coach appears to be a Dean clerestory.

(Great Western Trust)

A nice pre-war shot of No. 4034 *Queen Adelaide* (BRD)
as it ascends Dainton with a down stopping service.
(Great Western Trust)

A down fast service to Birmingham via Oxford is seen here at Ealing, hauled by a rather dirty No. 4018 *Knight of the Grand Cross* (WSR) in July 1945. Both the locomotive and stock are in typical wartime condition.
(C. G. Stuart/Great Western Trust)

Not the sharpest of pictures, but an interesting working shows No. 4014 *Knight of the Bath* (WSR) passing through Ludlow in September 1945 with a special troop train which was carrying American servicemen. No. 4014 did not last for much longer, being withdrawn in June 1946.
(C. G. Stuart/Great Western Trust)

A fast up service from Swindon speeds through Ealing in April 1946, hauled by Swindon-based No. 4022 (previously *Belgian Monarch*). It is coupled to 3,500 gallon Collett tender No. 2253.

(C. G. Stuart/Great Western Trust)

Another shot at Ealing, again taken in April 1946, shows No. 4017 *Knight of Liége* (SWN) passing through on an up fast service. It is coupled to Collett 4,000 gallon tender No. 2416. No. 4017 was one of the Saints never to be fitted with outside steam pipes, and was withdrawn in November 1949.

(C. G. Stuart/Great Western Trust)

Some last-minute attention to 4043 *Princes Henry* (BRD) as it waits at Paddington, probably in early 1946, with a down West of England service. The locomotive is in fully lined green livery and in ex-works condition after a General repair at Swindon.

(C. G. Stuart/Great Western Trust)

A nice pre-nationalisation shot of No. 4057 *Princess Elizabeth* (SWN) on a west of England service.
(Great Western Trust)

No. 4036 *Queen Elizabeth* (WEY) is seen here backing onto an up service at Weymouth on 20 August 1948.
(Great Western Trust)

An up fast service from Oxford to Paddington approaches
Kennington Junction, south of Oxford, in September 1946, hauled
by Oxford-based No. 4052 *Princess Beatrice*.

(C. G. Stuart/Great Western Trust)

No. 4060 *Princess Eugenie* (WSR) passes Old Oak Lane Halt on 23 January 1947 with the 11.15 am service from Paddington to Birmingham.
(C. G. Stuart/Great Western Trust)

No. 4057 *Princess Elizabeth* (SWN) stands at Paddington on 30 April 1947 after arriving with a service from Bristol.
(M. Yarwood/Great Western Trust)

An unidentified semi-fast service, comprising five coaches
and a van, is pictured here near Westbury in June 1947, hauled
by No. 4038 *Queen Berengaria* (WEY).
(Great Western Trust)

An up stopping service from Kingswear, hauled by a scruffy looking No. 4012 *Knight of the Thistle* (NA), waits to depart from Churston in May 1947. This locomotive was never fitted with outside steam pipes and was withdrawn from Newton Abbot on 21 October 1949.
(F. M. Gates/Great Western Trust)

No. 4047 *Princess Louise* (BRD) stands in the yard at Cardiff Canton in around 1947. It is fitted with a speedometer, but was another Star never to be fitted with outside steam pipes. It was withdrawn on 30 July 1951.
(F. M. Gates/Great Western Trust)

No. 4042 *Prince Albert* (BRD) looks to be in a rather run-down condition as it stands at Taunton with an express freight in around 1949. It received its elbow steam pipes as late as May 1948, but at this point has not yet received its smokebox number plate. It was withdrawn on November 1951. Prince Albert had succeeded his elder brother, King Edward VIII, after his abdication in 1936, becoming King George VI on 11 December 1936.

(Great Western Trust)

An un-named No. 4026 is pictured here running tender first at an unidentified location in around 1948. Notice the TN (Taunton) stencilled on the front frame and also the 'Star Class' painted on the centre splasher. It is running here with Collett 4,000 gallon tender No. 2885. No. 4026 was withdrawn on 20 February 1950 and was one of the Stars that were never fitted with a smokebox number plate.
(Great Western Trust)

An interesting picture of an un-named No. 4026 (83B), taken at Bristol Temple Meads on 1 June 1948. It is coupled to Collett 4,000 gallon tender No. 2887, which is lettered 'BRITISH RAILWAYS' in shaded block capitals. This was used for a short while on some tenders prior to the introduction of the British Railways Lion and Wheel emblem.
(C. G. Stuart/Great Western Trust)

A great shot of No. 4049 *Princess Maud* (OXF) as it passes West Ealing on 20 June 1948 with a fast service to Oxford. It is fitted with Castle type outside steam pipes.
(C. G. Stuart/Great Western Trust)

No. 4062 *Malmesbury Abbey* (SWN) and an unidentified Castle are seen here at Westbourne Park on 28 July 1948 double heading a fast service to Bristol.
(C. G. Stuart/Great Western Trust)

A down fast service to Cheltenham and Gloucester speeds past Westbourne Park on 30 July 1948, hauled by No. 4062 *Malmesbury Abbey* (SWN). No. 4062 was fitted with outside steam pipes as late as March 1950.
(C. G. Stuart/Great Western Trust)

Looking majestic, No. 4007 *Swallowfield Park* (WOS) is turned at Ranelagh Bridge in around 1948. Originally named *Rising Star* it was renamed *Swallowfield Park* in May 1937, and was fitted with elbow outside steam pipes in May 1947.

(J. Ashman/Great Western Trust)

A service from Worcester to Paddington is pictured here at Ruscombe on 8 May 1949, hauled by No. 4052 *Princess Beatrice* (WOS).
(M. Yarwood/Great Western Trust)

Pictured at Bristol Bath Road, its home shed, on 12 June 1949, is No. 4043 *Prince Henry*. It has been fitted with a speedometer and is running with Collett 4,000 gallon tender No. 2595. Many of the Stars looked run-down during this period.
(Great Western Trust)

An up service from Worcester to Paddington, hauled by No. 4051 *Princess Helena* (WOS), stands at the south end of the up platform at Oxford on 24 June 1949.
(F. M. Gates/Great Western Trust)

No. **4021** *British Monarch* (81F) is seen here at Evesham on 14 May 1949 with an up stopping service. It was fitted with elbow steam pipes as late as July 1948. The large screw reverser can also be seen to good effect.
(F. M. Gates/Great Western Trust)

Looking immaculate after a Heavy General repair at Swindon, No. 4040 *Queen Boadicea* stand in the yard at Swindon Works on 12 August 1949. It has been fitted with a smokebox number plate but has its home shed Salop stencilled on the front frame.

(Great Western Trust)

No. 4060 *Princess Eugenie* (BRD) stands at Salisbury with a Bristol service on 26 August 1949. It is coupled here to Collett 4,000 gallon tender No. 2713.

(W. Gilburt/Great Western Trust)

No. 4062 *Malmesbury Abbey* (82C) is pictured here at Swindon on 30 April 1950 coupled to Hawksworth straight sided 4,000 gallon tender No. 4056. It ran with this tender from 4 April until 1 May 1950. From April 1952 until January 1953 it ran with Hawksworth tender No. 4014, and then from July 1955 until its withdrawal in November 1956 it was coupled to yet another Hawksworth, this time No. 4046. The locomotive is fitted with a speedometer, and notice also the Collett style housing fitted to the screw reverse ahead of the cab.

(E. Mountford/Great Western Trust)

The 10.40 am through service from Wolverhampton to Brighton and Hastings comprising Southern stock is seen here at Reading on 27 May 1950, hauled by No. 4053 *Princess Alexandra* (84A). Its Collett 4,000 gallon tender No. 2574 is lettered 'BRITISH RAILWAYS'.

(Great Western Trust)

A down fast service from Worcester to
Paddington approaches Radley in June 1950,
hauled by No. 4051 *Princess Helena* (85A).
(M. Yarwood/Great Western Trust)

An up service from Worcester to Paddington, hauled by
No. 4007 *Swallowfield Park* (85A), is seen here at Kennington,
south of Oxford, in June 1950.

(M. Yarwood/Great Western Trust)

The 1.18 pm service to Bristol is seen here at Paddington on 31 May 1950, hauled by an un-named No. 4022 (previously *Belgian Monarch*) (82C)
(C. G. Stuart/Great Western Trust)

No. 4028 (ex-*Roumanian Monarch*) is seen here at Salisbury on 1 July 1950. It is in its final condition, with lined green livery, Star Class on middle splasher, inside steam pipes, smokebox number plate and 82D Westbury shed plate. The Collett 4,000 gallon tender is No. 2756. Notice the circular blanking plate on the smokebox side, which suggests that the boiler had previously been used on a locomotive with outside steam pipes. It was withdrawn from service on 9 November 1951.
(W. Gilburt/Great Western Trust)

Pictured in the works yard at Swindon on 1 May 1950 is No. 4022 (previously *Belgian Monarch*) after a Heavy General repair. It has the Grange type chimney and is fitted with a speedometer. It is coupled to Collett 4,000 gallon tender No. 4017 that has the short-lived 'BRITISH RAILWAYS' on its side. Notice SWN, its home shed, painted on the front frame. This was its last major repair, as it was withdrawn from Swindon on 14 February 1952.

(E. Mountford/Great Western Trust)

No. 4041 *Prince of Wales* (BRD) pulls away from Stratford-upon-Avon on 5 August 1950 with the 10.35 am Saturdays only service from Paignton to Wolverhampton.
(Great Western Trust)

No. 4025 (previously *Italian Monarch*) is pictured here at Plymouth Laira in 1950. It was withdrawn from Wolverhampton Stafford Road on 4 August of the same year.
(Great Western Trust)

A great shot of No. 4033 *Queen Victoria* on the 1.20 pm service from Taunton to Paddington, taking water at Foxes Wood water troughs at Keynsham on 2 September 1950.
(Great Western Trust)

Another picture shows No. 4033 *Queen Victoria*, this time at Powderham on 20 February 1951. It is on the three-coach Torquay portion of a Penzance to Birmingham service. The Penzance portion will be added at Exeter.
(P. M. Alexander/Great Western Trust)

Looking to be in a run-down condition No. 4020 *Knight Commander* (82A) stands in the yard at Newton Abbot in February 1951. It retains its original box inside cylinder cover; it was fitted with elbow steam pipes as late as March 1949 and is coupled here to Collett 4,000 gallon tender No. 2848. No. 4020 was withdrawn from service on 21 March 1951.
(Great Western Trust)

No. 4058 *Princess Augusta* (84A) is seen here at Bentley Heath on a Paddington to Wolverhampton service. It is coupled to Hawksworth 4,000 gallon straight sided tender No. 4049 that it retained until withdrawal on 16 April 1951.
(C. F. Oldham/Great Western Trust)

No. 4042 *Prince Albert* (82A) stands in the yard at Bristol Bath Road on 22 April 1951. It is in its final condition with elbow steam pipes, speedometer and smokebox number and shed plates. It is coupled here to Collett 4,000 gallon tender No. 2897.
(Great Western Trust)

No. 4044 *Prince George* (84G) stands at Shrewsbury with an unidentified service, probably from the west of England, in May 1951.
(F. M. Gates/Great Western Trust)

No. 4007 *Swallowfield Park* (85A) backs out of Paddington after
working in with the 7.45 am service from Worcester in May 1951. It
was first allocated to Worcester in December 1935 and remained there
until its withdrawal on 3 September 1951. It was the last surviving
working member of the 1907 batch of Stars.
(C. G. Stuart/Great Western Trust)

No. 4033 *Queen Victoria* (82A) stands at Reading on 15 May 1951, just a month before its withdrawal on 14 June 1951. It is coupled to Collett 4,000 gallon tender No. 2771.
(F. M. Gates/Great Western Trust)

The sad end to No. 4018 *Knight of the Grand Cross*, seen here on the scrap line at Swindon on 19 June 1951. Built in April 1908, it was withdrawn from Wolverhampton Stafford Road on 23 April 1951 having completed 1,977,146 miles in service.
(F. M. Gates/Great Western Trust)

The up Merchant Venturer, the 4.35 pm service from Weston-super-Mare to Paddington, pulls into Bristol Temple Meads in June 1951, hauled by un-named No. 4028 (82D). This locomotive was never fitted with outside steam pipes and is seen here coupled to Collett 4,000 gallon tender No. 2756.

(Great Western Trust)

A fast service from Paddington to Bristol is pictured here at Cholsey in June 1951, hauled by No. 4060 *Princess Eugenie* (82A).

(M. Yarwood/Great Western Trust)

No. 4061 *Glastonbury Abbey* (84A) approaches Cheltenham via the Honeybourne and Cheltenham route on 17 April 1952 with a race special service from Birmingham to Cheltenham Racecourse Station.
(Great Western Trust)

No. 4060 *Princess Eugenie* (82A) is seen here at Salisbury shed yard in 1952 after working in with a service from Bristol.
(Great Western Trust)

The 09.15 am Sunday service from Cheltenham to Paddington, hauled by No. 4059 *Princess Patricia* (85B), passes Minety on 19 April 1952.
(Great Western Trust)

The 2.55 pm service from Paignton to Wolverhampton calls at Torquay, hauled by a rather grubby looking No. 4044 *Prince George* (84G) on 19 July 1952.
(J. Whitnall/Great Western Trust)

No. 4053 *Princess Alexandra* (84A) passes Oldfield Park on 10 June 1952 with a stopping service from Bristol to Swindon. The locomotive is on a running-in turn after a Heavy General repair at Swindon works. This was its last repair at Swindon as it was withdrawn from service on 12 July 1954.
(P. A. Fry/Great Western Trust)

No. 4049 *Princess Maud* (84A) pulls away from Shrewsbury on 28 August 1952 with the 2.35 pm service to Paddington. It had been fitted with Castle pattern steam pipes in February 1935.
(Brian Morrison)

The sad sight of No. 4023 (formerly *Danish Monarch*) in the cutting shop at Swindon on 16 September 1952. It was withdrawn from its home shed, Swansea Landore, on 12 July 1952. The GWR shed code LDR can just be seen on the running plate. The chalk number refers to the boiler No. 4978, and the writing on the cylinder seems to indicate that it should not be scrapped.
(E. Mountford/Great Western Trust)

No. 4049 *Princess Maud* (84A) stands at Reading on 17 June 1953 with what appears to be an up parcels service.
(F. M. Gates/Great Western Trust)

No. 4053 *Princess Alexandra* stands alongside the coaling plant at Wolverhampton Stafford Road, its home shed, on 15 March 1953. It is seen here in its final form coupled to Collett 4,000 gallon tender No. 2697. It had been fitted with the Castle pattern outside steam pipes during October 1933.

(M. Hale/Great Western Trust)

During this period the Stars were a popular locomotive on rail tours. Here No. 4056 *Princess Margaret* (82A) prepares to depart from a rather wet Exeter St Davids on 28 June 1953 with the return RCTS twenty-fith Anniversary Special from Exeter to Paddington. (Great Western Trust)

No. 4062 *Malmesbury Abbey* (82C) speeds through Badminton on 22 August 1954 with a Paddington to South Wales service. A month earlier it had left Swindon after a Heavy General repair; this was its last major repair at Swindon.
(Great Western Trust)

No. 4061 *Glastonbury Abbey* (84A) approaches the top of Hatton Bank on 21 June 1955 with a service to Wolverhampton. It was withdrawn on 8 January 1957.
(M. Hale/Great Western Trust)

No. 4061 *Glastonbury Abbey* (84A) minus both its smokebox and shed number plates and with its number painted on the front buffer beam, comes off the west loop at Foxhall Junction, Didcot, on 11 September 1955 with the Stephenson Locomotive Society Midland area 'Star Special' from Birmingham to Swindon, returning via Oxford and Stratford-upon-Avon.

(D. Luscombe/Great Western Trust)

Another shot of No. 4061 *Glastonbury Abbey* as it stands in the yard at Wolverhampton Stafford Road, its home shed, on 9 October 1955. It is coupled to Collett 4,000 gallon tender No. 4050. No. 4061 was withdrawn on 11 March 1957.

(M. Hale/Great Western Trust)

The last working Star, No. 4056 *Princess Margaret* (82A), is pictured here near Shrewsbury on 22 September 1956 with the Talyllyn Railway Preservation Society AGM special from Paddington to Towyn. The Star hauled the train between Paddington and Shrewsbury.

(Great Western Trust)

A more mundane duty for No. 4056 *Princess Margaret* (82A) as it departs from Swindon on 21 October 1956 with a four-coach down stopping service to Bristol. The locomotive was sadly withdrawn on 28 October 1957. (Great Western Trust)

A view of the cab layout of No. 4042 *Prince Albert*, pictured here withdrawn at Swindon in November 1951.

(Great Western Trust)

Visitors to Swindon works in the 1950s were nearly always taken to the stock shed to see No. 4003 *Lode Star* and Dean Goods 0-6-0 No. 2516, which were in store. No. 4003 is pictured here inside the stock shed, probably soon after its withdrawal on 18 July 1951. At this time it was running with Collett 4,000 gallon tender No. 2410, but for its subsequent preservation it was coupled to Churchward 3,500 gallon tender No. 1726 as seen here.

(E. Mountford/Great Western Trust)

APPENDIX

Diagrams

4-4-2 D	No 40 as built
4-6-0 H	Nos. 4001–20 non-superheated
4-6-0 J	No. 4010 Cole superheater
4-6-0 K	No. 4011 Swindon No. 1 superheater
4-6-0 M	No. 4012 Swindon No. 3 superheater
4-6-0 N	Nos. 4022–4030 no superheated
4-6-0 Q	Nos. 4031–4040 variant superheater
4-6-0 S	No. 4041 variant superheater, 15in cylinders
4-6-0 T	Nos. 4042–4045 same as S but with 14¼in cylinders
4-6-0 U	40XX variant superheater and 15in cylinders
4-6-0	A10 40XX same as U but with 4,000 gallon tenders.

The Stars were classified: D Red
British Railways power class: 5P

Swindon Works/Lot Numbers

Locomotive Nos.	Works Nos.	Lot No
40 (4000)	2168	161
4001–10	2229–2238	168
4011–20	2300–2309	173
4021–30	2365–2374	178
4031–40	2380–2389	180
4041–45	2536–2540	#195
4046–60	2572–2586	#199
4061–72	2915–2926	#217

Plates were not carried on these locomotives

No.	Name	Built	First Allocation	Final Allocation	Withdrawn	Final Mileage
40 (4000)	*North Star*	Mar 1906	Old Oak Common	Bath Road	Nov 1929	918,804 plus 1,426,356#
4001	*Dog Star*	Feb 1907	Old Oak Common	Bath Road	Jan 1934	1,234,777
4002	*Evening Star*	Mar 1907	Plymouth Laira	Old Oak Common	Jun 1935	1,184,039
4003	*Lode Star*	Mar 1907	Old Oak Common	Landore	Jul 1951	2,005,898
4004	*Morning Star*	Mar 1907	Plymouth Laira	Oxford	Apr 1948	1,875,324
4005	*Polar Star*	Mar 1907	Old Oak Common	Old Oak Common	Nov 1934	1,181,052
4006	*Red Star*	Apr 1907	Old Oak Common	Landore	Dec 1932	1,219.032
4007	*Rising Star*	Apr 1907	Old Oak Common	Worcester	Sept 1951	1,942,263
4008	*Royal Star*	May 1907	Plymouth Laira	Old Oak Common	Jun 1935	1,118,424
4009	*Shooting Star*	May 1907	Plymouth Laira	Plymouth Laira	Apr 1925	810,354 plus 1,164,297#
4010	*Western Star*	May 1907	Old Oak Common	Bath Road	Nov 1934	1,277,503
4011	*Knight of the Garter*	Mar 1908	Old Oak Common	Worcester	Nov 1932	1,053,580
4012	*Knight of the Thistle*	Mar 1908	Old Oak Common	Newton Abbot	Oct 1949	1,860,642
4013	*Knight of St Patrick*	Mar 1908	Old Oak Common	Chester	May 1950	1,814,680

No.	Name	Built	First Allocation	Final Allocation	Withdrawn	Final Mileage
4014	*Knight of the Bath*	Mar 1908	Cardiff Canton	Stafford Road	Jun 1946	1,766,634
4015	*Knight of St John*	Mar 1908	Bath Road	Swindon	Feb 1951	1,946,315
4016	*Knight of the Golden Fleece*	Apr 1908	Old Oak Common	Old Oak Common	Jul 1925	785,796 plus 1,186,663#
4017	*Knight of the Black Eagle*	Apr 1908	Old Oak Common	Swindon	Nov 1949	1.917,809
4018	*Knight of the Grand Cross*	Apr 1908	Old Oak Common	Stafford Road	Apr 1951	1,977,146
4019	*Knight Templar*	May 1908	Old Oak Common	Bath Road	Oct 1949	1,881,077
4020	*Knight Commander*	May 1908	Bath Road	Bath Road	Mar 1951	1,959,899
4021	*King Edward*	Jun 1909	Old Oak Common	Oxford	Oct 1952	1,034,975
4022	*King William*	Jun 1909	Old Oak Common	Swindon	Feb 1952	2,031,356
4023	*King George*	Jun 1909	Old Oak Common	Landore	Jul 1952	1,912,170
4024	*King James*	Jun 1909	Old Oak Common	Taunton	Feb 1935	1,309,581
4025	*King Charles*	Jul 1909	Old Oak Common	Stafford Road	Aug 1950	1,827,122
4026	*King Richard*	Sept 1909	Old Oak Common	Taunton	Jul 1950	1,887,903
4027	*King Henry*	Sept 1909	Old Oak Common	Landore	Oct 1934	1,121,371
4028	*King John*	Sept 1909	Old Oak Common	Westbury	Nov 1951	1,975,449
4029	*King Stephen*	Oct 1909	Old Oak Common	Stafford Road	Nov 1934	1,261,970
4030	*King Harold*	Oct 1909	Old Oak Common	Bath Road	May 1950	1,793,048
4031	*Queen Mary*	Oct 1910	Old Oak Common	Stafford Road	Jun 1951	1,882,165
4032	*Queen Alexandra*	Oct 1910	Plymouth Laira	Exeter	Dec 1925	755,427 plus 1,225,908#
4033	*Queen Victoria*	Nov 1910	Plymouth Laira	Bath Road	Jun 1951	1,812,013
4034	*Queen Adelaide*	Nov 1910	Old Oak Common	Swindon	Sept 1952	1,965,994
4035	*Queen Charlotte*	Nov 1910	Plymouth Laira	Bath Road	Oct 1951	1,999,038
4036	*Queen Elizabeth*	Dec 1910	Plymouth Laira	Swindon	Mar 1952	1,962,151
4037	*Queen Philippa*	Dec 1910	Plymouth Laira	Old Oak Common	Feb 1925	776,764 plus 1,652,958#
4038	*Queen Berengaria*	Jan 1911	Old Oak Common	Westbury	Apr 1952	1,994,758
4039	*Queen Matilda*	Feb 1911	Newton Abbot	Landore	Nov 1950	1,853,757
4040	*Queen Boadicea*	Mar 1911	Old Oak Common	Shrewsbury	Jun 1951	1,782,624
4041	*Prince of Wales*	Jun 1913	Plymouth Laira	Bath Road	Apr 1951	1,694,440
4042	*Prince Albert*	May 1913	Newton Abbot	Bath Road	Nov 1951	1,807,273
4043	*Prince Henry*	May 1913	Old Oak Common	Bath Road	Jan 1952	1,862,402
4044	*Prince George*	May 1913	Old Oak Common	Shrewsbury	Feb 1953	1,782,236
4045	*Prince John*	Jun 1913	Old Oak Common	Westbury	Nov 1950	1,716,935
4046	*Princess Mary*	May 1914	Old Oak Common	Shrewsbury	Nov 1951	1,612,680
4047	*Princess Louise*	May 1914	Plymouth Laira	Bath Road	Jul 1951	1,773,415
4048	*Princess Victoria*	May 1914	Stafford Road	Landore	Jan 1953	1,770,921
4049	*Princess Maud*	May 1914	Old Oak Common	Stafford Road	Jul 1953	1,683,157
4050	*Princess Alice*	Jun 1914	Stafford Road	Landore	Feb 1952	1,706,323
4051	*Princess Helena*	Jun 1914	Plymouth Laira	Worcester	Dec 1950	1,712,107
4052	*Princess Beatrice*	Jun 1914	Plymouth Laira	Shrewsbury	Jun 1953	1,684,251
4053	*Princess Alexandra*	Jun 1914	Old Oak Common	Stafford Road	Jul 1954	1,806,399
4054	*Princess Charlotte*	Jun 1914	Plymouth Laira	Plymouth Laira	Feb 1952	1,714,939
4055	*Princess Sophia*	Jul 1914	Old Oak Common	Swindon	Feb 1951	1,691,686
4056	*Princess Margaret*	Jul 1914	Stafford Road	Bath Road	Oct 1957	2,074,338
4057	*Princess Elizabeth*	Jul 1914	Stafford Road	Swindon	Feb 1952	1,791,922
4058	*Princess Auga*	Jul 1914	Stafford Road	Stafford Road	Apr 1951	1,648,601

No.	Name	Built	First Allocation	Final Allocation	Withdrawn	Final Mileage
4059	*Princess Patricia*	Jul 1914	Old Oak Common	Gloucester	Sept 1952	1,739,565
4060	*Princess Eugenie*	Jul 1914	Old Oak Common	Bath Road	Oct 1952	1,816,021
4061	*Glastonbury Abbey*	May 1922	Old Oak Common	Stafford Road	Mar 1957	1,550,800
4062	*Malmesbury Abbey*	May 1922	Plymouth Laira	Swindon	Nov 1956	1,612,472
4063	*Bath Abbey*	Nov 1922	Newton Abbot	Landore	Apr 1937	821,148 plus 1,001,686##
4064	*Reading Abbey*	Dec 1922	Old Oak Common	Bath Road	Feb 1937	738,703 plus 1,188,386##
4065	*Evesham Abbey*	Dec 1922	Exeter	Stafford Road	Mar 1939	810,737 plus 1,214,357##
4066	*Malvern Abbey*	Dec 1922	Stafford Road	Gloucester	Dec 1937	810,777 plus 1,060,724##
4067	*Tintern Abbey*	Jan 1923	Stafford Road	Weymouth	Sept 1940	940,219 plus 1,088,932##
4068	*Llanthony Abbey*	Jan 1923	Stafford Road	Stafford Road	Dec 1938	832,853 plus 1,047,102##
4069	*Margam Abbey*	Jan 1923	Stafford Road	Bath Road	Apr 1939	938,354 plus 1,158,893##
4070	*Neath Abbey*	Feb 1923	Stafford Road	Gloucester	Feb 1939	896,314 plus 1,161,961#
4071	*Cleeve Abbey*	Feb 1923	Old Oak Common	Bath Road	Sept 1938	835,788 plus 1,082,935#
4072	*Tresco Abbey*	Feb 1923	Old Oak Common	Taunton	Dec 1937	825,283 plus 1,143,594#

#Separate mileages shown for Star and Castle.

##Rebuilt as Castle Class and renumbered 5083–5092 , separate mileages shown as Star and Castle.

No 40 was named *North Star* in September 1906. It was renumbered 4000 on 28 December 1912, and was withdrawn from Bath Road in July 1929 for conversion to a Castle.

No 4009 *Shooting Star* was withdrawn from Plymouth Laira in April 1925 for conversion to a Castle.

No 4016 *Knight of the Golden Fleece* was withdrawn from Old Oak Common in July 1925 for conversion to a Castle.

No 4032 *Queen Alexandra* was withdrawn from Exeter in December 1925 for conversion to a Castle.

No 4037 *Queen Philippa* was withdrawn from Old Oak Common in February 1925 for conversion to a Castle.

Name Changes

No 4007 renamed *Swallowfield Park* in May 1937.

No 4017 renamed *Knight of Liége* in August 1914.

No 4021 renamed *The British Monarch* in June 1927, *British Monarch* in October 1927. Name retained until withdrawal.

No 4022 renamed *The Belgian Monarch* in June 1927, *Belgian Monarch* in October 1927. Name removed May 1940.

No 4023 renamed *The Danish Monarch* in July 1927, *Danish Monarch* in October 1927. Name removed November 1940.

No 4024 renamed *The Dutch Monarch* in September 1927, *Dutch Monarch* in November 1927.

No 4025 renamed *Italian Monarch* in October 1927. Name removed June 1940.

No 4026 renamed *The Japanese Monarch* in July 1927, *Japanese Monarch* in October 1927. Name removed January 1941.

No 4027 renamed *The Norwegian Monarch* in July 1927, *Norwegian Monarch* in October 1927. Withdrawn October 1934.

No 4028 renamed *The Roumanian Monarch* in July 1927, *Roumanian Monarch* in October 1927. Name removed November 1940.

No 4029 renamed *The Spanish Monarch* in July 1927, *Spanish Monarch* in October 1927. Withdrawn November 1934.

No 4030 renamed *The Swedish Monarch* in July 1927, *Swedish Monarch* in October 1927.Name removed November 1940.

After the removal of the names the words 'Star Class' were painted on the centre splashers.

No 4048 *Princess Victoria* was temporarily named *Princess Mary* on 28 February 1922 on the occasion of the Royal Wedding.

No 4066 was renamed *Sir Robert Horne* in May 1935 and *Viscount Horne* in August 1937.

No 4069 was renamed *Westminster Abbey* in May 1923.